The decolonization of Africa

84

Pg 72
74

The decolonization of Africa

David Birmingham
University of Kent

Ohio University Press • Athens

Published in the United States of America by Ohio University Press, Athens, Ohio 45701

First published in 1995 by UCL Press
The name of University College London (UCL) is a registered trade mark used by UCL Press with the consent of the owner.

Library of Congress Cataloging-in-Publication Data

Birmingham, David.
    The decolonization of Africa / David Birmingham.
      p.   cm.
    Includes bibliographical references and index.
    ISBN 0-8214-1153-5 (pbk.)
      1. Decolonization—Africa. 2. Nationalism—Africa—History—20th century. 3. Africa—History—20th century. 4. Africa—Relations—Europe. 5. Europe—Relations—Africa. I. Title.
    DT31.B5   1996
    960.3—dc20   95-41640
                                                             CIP
ISBN: 0-8214-1153-5

Typeset in Palatino and Gill Sans.
Printed and bound by
Page Bros (Norwich) Ltd, England.

Contents

Acknowledgements

This book is dedicated to the people of Africa who offered me much warm hospitality as a travelling historian. In northern Africa my memory dwells on the ancient and ornate city of Lepcis Magna, home of Rome's only African emperor, and on the elegant Moroccan harbour of Tangier, which the Portuguese gave to Britain as part of a dowry for Charles II's queen. In western Africa a deep impression was made on me by merchants who carried salt from the mines of the Sahara and gave me a lift from the old empire of Mali to the modern colony of Ghana. I also cycled round Africa's largest market in the Nigerian city of Kano and visited by boat the magnificent but tragic French slave island of Gorée. Missionaries were ever welcoming, but those who ran the Nigerian leper colony were tragically destroyed in the Biafran war. In eastern Africa the emperor of Ethiopia hosted a conference on the origins of man. In Kenya soldiers were seen to be actively engaged in politics both during the Mau Mau emergency and in the more recent aftermath of an attempted military coup. Watching the experiments with single-party democracy in Tanzania bring new hope to Africa's peasants, and exploring the old Arab city of Zanzibar and its clove plantations, were some of the privileges of a travelling teacher. In west-central Africa, as a visiting professor at Yaoundé, in the French sphere of educational influence, at Kinshasa in the Belgian sphere, and at Luanda in the Portuguese sphere, I learnt much from students about their struggles and aspirations in the aftermath of decolonization. Students in Katanga, in 1972, mourned the death of Kwame Nkrumah, Africa's first modern hero. In southern

ACKNOWLEDGEMENTS

Africa inspecting Mozambique's provincial archives during the truce at the end of the colonial war, and attending the ceremonial transfer of power in Zimbabwe, powerfully conveyed the excitement that liberation brought to Africa.

The genesis of this essay was an attempt to use Africa as a case study for training British students in the skills of the historian. I owe a deep debt of gratitude to the historians of Africa who have been my teachers, colleagues, students and friends over the years. This book, however, is naturally and properly an outsider's very personal interpretation of decolonization with its own choice of themes and ideas, its own perception of heroes and martyrs, and above all its own analysis of the varied and complex process that made decolonization in Africa a fascinating subject for historical research.

Introduction

The decolonization of Africa was one of the turning points in the history of the post-war world. It captured the imagination of a new generation of idealists who enthusiastically proclaimed their belief in racial equality and individual liberty. The liberation of Africa from European rule followed on the heels of the independence gained by India and other colonies in Asia. The struggle for political freedom by the peoples of Africa also helped to open the way for the civil rights movement in North America. In the 1950s new and relatively young leaders, Kwame Nkrumah in west Africa and Nelson Mandela in South Africa, stood in solidarity with Jawaharlal Nehru, the prime minister of India, and Martin Luther King, the apostle of black freedom in the United States. In the year 1960 no fewer than 17 former African colonies became independent members of the United Nations. These included Nigeria, Britain's densely populated west African territory; Somalia, the last Italian province in east Africa; Zaire, the giant Belgian colony in central Africa; and almost all of the French possessions in western, central and eastern Africa. The retreat of the tide of European imperialism seemed to be almost as rapid as its rise had been 75 years earlier. Yet the course of decolonization was not always smooth. Nkrumah spent only a short time in prison for seditiously questioning the British right to rule Africa and was released to become the prime minister of Ghana. Mandela, on the other hand, was charged with treason when he challenged the white monopoly of power in South Africa. He was locked away on a prison island and it was nearly 30 years before his carefully modulated democratic ideals

1

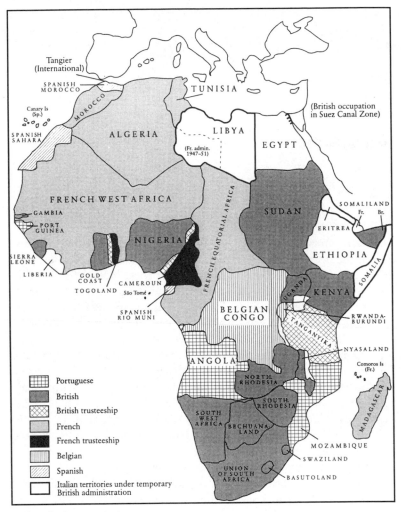

Colonial Africa in 1946

could be heard. The 1960 burst of decolonization was the central and most dramatic episode in a long process of political change that affected the whole of Africa, from Cairo to the Cape, and has lasted throughout the twentieth century. Decolonization was the mirror image of the colonization that had slowly brought European domination to Africa in the nineteenth century.

The colonization of Africa by foreigners had gained momentum throughout the course of the nineteenth century. It culminated in the carving up of the continent by seven European powers. The most influential of these drafted maps in Berlin in 1885 and agreed to more or less respect each others' spheres of influence. They did not, however, consult the people of Africa. Indeed, they sent small armies to Africa in order to turn the boundaries on their maps into frontiers on the ground. Owners of the land who resisted the arrival of the self-styled forces of "civilization" were to be "pacified" by conquest. Eventually Portugal, Spain, Italy, Germany, Belgium, France and Britain carved out 54 territories that were later to become nations.

The partition of Africa did not create a set of uniform colonies each resembling the other in a constitutional stereotype. On the contrary, the establishment of colonial rule was varied and pragmatic. The differences were to be found not only between empires but within empires. European nations had claimed spheres of influence in Africa since the fifteenth century and had tried to protect their preferred zones of commerce. A few early traders settled in Africa, creating merchant enclaves, fathering extended families, and introducing European customs of law and religion. In the nineteenth century a new type of colony was created in which the settlers were black immigrants, former slaves sent back to Africa from America and Europe. Their descendants, locally born Creoles who blended their African heritage with their adopted European culture, formed a social and political elite in several colonies of western Africa. A quite different type of colonizer arriving in Africa consisted of free immigrants who escaped from Europe in search of cheap land. These white settlers resembled those going to Australia or America, but in Africa they faced a much greater resistance to their conquering pretensions. In much of tropical Africa local farmers and their armed rulers kept white settlers out, but in northern and southern Africa settlers conquered both land and the people whom they forced to work for them. In the north the settlers of Algeria aspired to unite their territory with France, much as plantation settlers in Ireland had united their colony with Britain. In the south, by contrast, settlers in the Cape aspired to loosen the imperial ties and win "dominion status" with a local white government directly responsible to the British crown.

Colonies in Africa were not only lands of immigration and settlement but also territories that were conquered and ruled by foreign governments. One type of foreign rule was a "protectorate", in which an indigenous African government remained more or less intact but its foreign affairs were taken over by an imperial power in Europe. In tropical Africa some local chiefs, and also more powerful paramount chiefs, saw their territories incorporated into protectorates, which effectively became colonies ruled by European administrators. Colonial powers that did not wish to devote exchequer resources to financing the administration of their conquest colonies sometimes issued imperial charters to private companies that were given the right to extract wealth in exchange for the responsibility of maintaining "law and order". Zimbabwe was governed by such a company until 1923, as was part of Mozambique until 1940. The colonies that Germany conquered in 1885 were later confiscated after the First World War and the League of Nations issued "mandates" for their administration by neighbouring colonial powers. After the Second World War nominal supervision of the partitioned German empire was given to the United Nations under the term "trusteeship". The role of the United Nations in overseeing the interests of indigenous peoples was not very effective in protecting human rights and liberties. It did, however, signal that colonizers theoretically had responsibilities for the welfare of their subjects. When such responsibilities appeared to outweigh the economic and strategic benefits of holding colonial possessions the option of decolonization became more attractive.

The earliest phases of decolonization took place almost before the colonial conquests had been completed. Already in the nineteenth century black settlers in Liberia and white settlers in the Cape were deemed by America and Britain to be capable of running their own internal affairs without cost to the colonizing power. After the First World War the authority of the "protected" king of Egypt was extended to grant him semi-independence, although British troops remained on his soil, to the dismay of nationalist politicians. In the 1940s the independence of the emperor of Ethiopia was recognized by Britain, although British, and later American, influence remained strong. Soon afterwards the Italian empire in Africa was gradually decolonized, although without any explicit recognition that this was creating a precedent for Britain, France, Belgium and Portugal. After the Second World War, with its rhetoric of freedom and self-determination in Europe, and its legacy of decolonization in Asia, the debate over independence for Africa could not be silenced.

Britain was the first imperial power to acknowledge that it could benefit by granting self-government to its colonies. It also calculated that a negotiated transfer of power would avoid the need to defend the colonies by force of arms when frustrated nationalist claims for independence led to violent protest. The economic and strategic benefits of holding the colonies, it was thought, could be maintained without the political and financial cost of direct control. These beliefs were challenged, however, in Kenya, where a small settler community provocatively demanded special treatment for its interests. Britain was forced to go to war to protect its white kith and kin. This war finally convinced all shades of British opinion that political decolonization accompanied by economic partnership was the only viable way of maintaining European influence in Africa. France, Belgium and Portugal eventually followed the same road, although at different speeds. Each, however, was involved in a serious armed confrontation with its colonial subjects before recognizing that the old colonial nexus was not viable, nor indeed necessary to metropolitan interests.

In the 1950s it was tacitly and naïvely assumed that African nationalism was a homogeneous ideological and political force that was pushing Europe into decolonization and was ready to don the mantle of state government. But the precept of common interests among colonial leaders was very far from the truth. In each of the colonies anti-colonialism provided a nationalist bandwagon onto which politicians of every persuasion were required to climb to achieve credibility. The leaders, however, had wider political agendas for postcolonial transformation. They sought support in the seething complexity of colonial societies splintered by class, ethnicity and belief, which foreigners so readily simplified into black and white. The new politicians faced a severe challenge in creating decision-making institutions. The departing colonial governors believed that the multiparty system of democracy that had returned to northwestern Europe after the dismembering of Hitler's empire would be appropriate for Africa too. In practice, the first generation of African governments came more closely to resemble the military dictatorships and one-party regimes of southern and eastern Europe. Colonialism had provided little experience of creative dialogue between opponents. Instead, it had used an authoritarian tradition for allocating scarce resources with a scant regard for equity. Democracy was not one of the legacies of empire in Africa.

A legacy of colonialism that did survive was geographical division and a striking feature of decolonization was the lack of change that it brought to the map of Africa. Colonial Africa in 1946 had much the same shape as independent Africa in 1995. With very few exceptions the boundaries that had been drawn so arbitrarily by the Victorians were retained two generations later by Africa's nationalist politicians. Indeed, it can be argued that the central feature of nationalism in any African country was the common desire to oppose the colonial rulers within their colonial frontiers. This anti-colonial nationalism, with rare exceptions, was not replaced by any broader forms of national awakening that transcended the frontiers of the old "scramble for Africa". The Somali people, it is true, tried to create a greater Somali nation after decolonization, but they could not bring into one fold their brethren scattered in Kenya, Ethiopia and Djibouti. Even the union of former British and former Italian Somali peoples was unsuccessful, despite their cultural and linguistic uniformity. Elsewhere similar attempts to erase colonial frontiers failed. Eritrea was absorbed by Ethiopia in the 1960s, but it rebelled to gain internationally recognized independence in the 1990s within frontiers mapped out by Italy in the 1890s. Senegal repeatedly tried to absorb the independent river-republic of Gambia, which ran through its territory, but never with more than limited success. Morocco marched into the Sahara to lay claim to former Spanish territory, but Algeria protested and supported a movement seeking recognition for an independent republic of Western Sahara. The one frontier that the new rulers did abolish was in Cameroun where part of the British Cameroons became a province of ex-French Cameroun. Ironically, the nationalists were restoring the old German colonial unity.

The new rulers not only preserved the frontiers of their colonial adversaries but also frequently hitched their postcolonial fortunes to the former colonizers. Most French territories became part of a francophone community chaired by the president of France, who kept a close political grip on African affairs. The two French federations of western Africa and equatorial Africa were politically dismembered and the individual territories were directly linked to Paris. Limited changes in international patronage enabled France to extend its influence to ex-Spanish Guinea and to ex-Belgian Rwanda. The English-speaking territories, with a few exceptions, joined a somewhat looser "commonwealth of nations" that was ceremonially presided over by the queen of England, although common diplomatic and military policy was eroded to a much greater extent than in French-speaking Africa. The influence of both Britain and France remained significant even when former colonies fell temporarily into the hands of tyrants, as happened in both the Central African Republic and Uganda. In the Portuguese colonies, by contrast, the surviving influence of the old colonial mother country was more limited. Although the Portuguese language remained the language of politics in Angola and Mozambique, foreign affairs fell increasingly under the influence of the superpowers. The last phase of decolonization became tied up with the Cold War as America and Russia fought a destructive "war by proxy" in Angola after their departure from Vietnam.

One of the penetrating cultural transformations brought to Africa was the acceptance of colonial languages as the languages of administration and justice in most of Africa's successor states. In a few of the emerging republics the ruling classes even preferred French, Portuguese or English in their social and political discourse and allowed their children to grow up ignorant of traditional vernaculars. Education, especially higher education, remained predominantly in the European mould, with European textbooks and teachers. A cultural influence even more pervasive than language and education was colonial religion. Christianity spread far beyond the colonial cities to affect the lives of rural peoples who still clung to their own languages and customs. When white political commissioners withdrew from Africa, many white missionaries remained and were supported by increasing numbers of black Christians. The decolonization of political institutions was often relatively rapid, but the minds of many Africans continued to work on colonial assumptions, making cultural, emotional and intellectual decolonization difficult for the heirs of empire.

The financial legacies of colonialism were also far reaching. In a few places decolonization brought the virtual disappearance of the monetary system, but for most independent Africans coins and bank notes had become a permanent feature of a wage and trade economy. For some, indeed, the coinage remained effectively colonial, controlled by external bankers and supported by exports to Europe on terms chosen by white consumers rather than by black producers. Under colonialism the terms of trade offered to individual farmers had often been ungenerous but no alternative outlets were available to them. The cost of credit had also been exorbitant and the penalties for defaulting brought draconian punishment. After independence whole nations found the terms of trade loaded against them and multinational agreements offered only limited protection. Nations found also that credit to the poor was expensive and the terms on which it was offered severely limited their economic freedoms of choice. Africa had to pay dearly for the foreign services in shipping, insurance and communications, which it was unable to provide for itself. When the Arab nations succeeded, as the African ones did not, in breaking the colonial nexus and determining for themselves the price of their exported oil, Africa was victimized yet again as a consumer which could ill afford to pay a fivefold price increase for its petroleum. African nations found their debts steeply mounting and the International Monetary Fund intervened to supervise their accounting and dictate their fiscal policies.

The most direct form of foreign influence to survive in Africa was neither cultural nor financial but military. The new states bought their weapons and training programmes from former colonial rulers or from other powers interested in gaining influence in the region. They also sought direct military help when facing crises. Britain and France gave overt and covert military help to their chosen political heirs when the social contracts between politicians and people appeared to be broken and rebellions threatened. In some cases politicians who could not depend on military support from former colonial patrons borrowed regiments from third parties, or recruited paid international mercenaries, to enhance their authority and repel foreign and domestic opponents. Not surprisingly, soldiers came to see themselves as the arbiters of independence and all too frequently took power into their own hands. This outcome had not been foreseen during the decolonizing process. The last phase of colonial politics had been largely concerned with the writing of sophisticated constitutions for the replacement of colonial regimes by democratic ones. Democracy, however, did not instantly take root and the immediate political legacy of colonialism was too often sternly authoritarian and even arbitrary.

CHAPTER ONE

Nationalism and self-government in northern Africa

Northern Africa stretches from the Spanish fishing grounds off the Western Sahara to the Italian colonies of the Eritrean highlands above the Red Sea. At the end of the Middle Ages northern Africa maintained close contact with Portugal, Castile, Aragon, Genoa and the Byzantine empire, while in the sixteenth century most of the region fell under the Turkish influence of the Ottoman empire. In the the nineteenth century northern Africa was parcelled out into eight European-ruled territories. Unlike much of tropical Africa, northern Africa attracted significant numbers of foreign immigrants. Most of these came from the opposite shore of the Mediterranean and settled in farming and trading communities not dissimilar to the communities created in the region 2,000 years earlier by European immigrants from the Greek city-states and the Roman empire. The modern settler colonies, however, only lasted for about 100 years. In the second half of the twentieth century most immigrants returned to the northern shores of the Mediterranean, sometimes followed by significant numbers of North Africans who became *gastarbeiter* in the prospering new economic community founded by Europe in 1957, just when the colonizers were beginning to leave Africa. The first of the north African territories to regain its independence of action after the imposition of European domination was Egypt.

During the First World War Britain had transformed its three decades of financial control over the kingdom of Egypt into a formal protectorate. This enabled it to assume full domination of the country while adjacent Arab territories, in the Turkish empire, were nominally

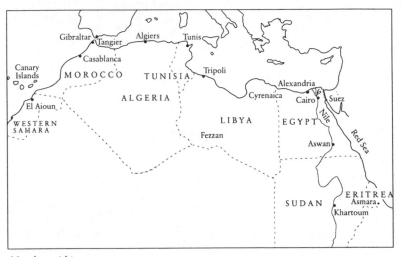

Northern Africa

linked to Germany. In 1922 Britain felt that its strategic hold on the Middle East was secure enough to end the protectorate over Egypt, although independence was on restricted terms. In particular, the interests of the million foreign residents in Egypt – mainly Greeks, Italians, Armenians and others who formed a tenth of the Egyptian population and a majority of its wealthier residents – remained under the protection of a British high commissioner. Nominally Egypt was ruled by the king and his prime minister, but the uncrowned high commissioner retained authority for foreign affairs, defence and the security of the Suez Canal. Decolonization, in Egypt as elsewhere, was only to be granted in carefully controlled stages.

The economic legacy of British control lay in the cotton fields. Britain had encouraged the growing of cotton to the exclusion of crops that were potentially more useful or valuable to the Egyptians, and had insisted that it be exported raw to the mills of Lancashire rather than processed locally for the benefit of the Egyptian industrial economy. It was a primary concern of Britain, and indeed of other colonial rulers of African territories, to try to ensure that the transfer of political power did not undermine the inexpensive supply of colonial-type raw materials and the profitable sale of finished products to former colonies. Thus, while Egyptian nationalists aspired to develop their own energy resources by damming the Nile and to spin their own cotton for their own textile industry, Britain endeavoured to restrict such bids for economic independence. The confrontation over economic decolonization, however, was postponed by the Second World War, during which British interests in Egypt were, as in the First World War, as much strategic as commercial.

After the Second World War three political traditions tried to win dominance in Egypt and restore the nationalist agenda of full political, military and economic independence. At first the liberals of the parliamentary monarchy that had governed after 1922 recovered their political role, but they were somewhat tarnished by their history of compromise with the foreign business interests that propped up a cosmopolitan (and allegedly decadent) royal court flaunting its wealth while the poor went hungry. A rival tradition, fostered by Muslim brotherhoods, wished to proclaim the supremacy of Egyptian cultural traditions and adopt a patriotic and puritanical agenda that excluded from public life all aliens and their Westernized Egyptian clients. The third political tradition grew up among a new class of young army officers. They had been recruited among "Arab" lower-middle-class Egyptian nationals rather than among upper-class white Egyptians, but they had been educated in English and trained in Western military traditions. Their political agenda involved challenging both the court with its culture of inequality and privilege, and also the Muslim brotherhoods with their backward-looking attachment to tradition. For Egypt to make real progress towards nationwide prosperity the officers also aspired to reduce the quasi-colonial domination of Britain and diversify foreign economic partnerships.

The military gained power in 1952 through a *coup d'état* that gradually became a revolution. The soldiers were acclaimed by crowds who, shortly before, had rioted in front of the colonial villas, cabarets and banks of Cairo. Their vision of decolonization was linked to a programme of industrialization that would turn peasants into industrial workers and give Egypt the standard of living hitherto enjoyed by Lancashire. Without coal or oil, however, they needed hydroelectricity on a large scale and this required a grandiose plan for the damming of the Nile. The Egyptian business class, frightened by the growing radicalism of the nationalist agenda and the prospect of crown properties becoming nationalized, had been moving their assets out of the country; domestic capital could not be raised on a

11

scale sufficient to implement the grand vision of economic transformation. The revolutionary government therefore looked abroad for
investment capital and initially found it in the United States. Very rapidly, however, the Western offer to invest in Egypt's revolutionary
agenda was withdrawn when the United States realized that the inde-
pendent-minded Egyptian leaders were also conducting business with
America's Cold War rivals in the Soviet empire. In 1956 the politics of
energy, industry and the Nile dam became linked to the politics of
foreign influence over the Suez Canal.

Egypt's Suez Canal, built by France and guarded by Britain, was
internationally important for two reasons. First, it provided the short-
est strategic route between Europe and Asia for military vessels patrol-
ling the colonial and ex-colonial spheres of influence surrounding the
Indian Ocean. Secondly, it provided the cheapest means of shipping
petroleum from the great Iranian and Saudi oil fields to the Mediterranean and North Atlantic ports. Foreign ownership, management and
defence of the canal caused each generation of Egyptian nationalists
to feel that their independence was only partial and that British troops
defending the canal were a constant threat to their sovereignty. This
unresolved antagonism was exacerbated in 1956 when Britain joined
America in refusing to finance the building of a high dam on the Nile.
The soldier-politicians decided to solve two outstanding problems at
once by nationalizing the canal and using revenue from the canal to
pay the interest on loans to build the dam. Although the nationalization was properly conducted according to approved financial custom,
the challenge to British and French supremacy in the area was unacceptable and they conspired to recover the canal by military means,
and if possible to replace the radical nationalist government with a
more pliant one.

The Anglo-French invasion of Egypt in October 1956 did not
achieve its objectives. On the contrary, it weakened both of the leading
colonial powers, strengthened the influence of the two super-powers
in Africa, and made the Egyptian nationalists into heroes throughout
much of the colonial world. Gamal Abd al-Nasser, the Egyptian president, became a name reviled in the Europe he had shamed, but idol-
ized in Africa where colonial subjects began tuning into Egyptian
radio broadcasts. They learnt about decolonization and the retreat of
empire, about the aid programmes established by the Soviet Union,
and about the way in which the United States had determined that

Africa should be handed back to the Africans and had forced Britain and France to end their military invasion. A chastised Britain was compelled to ration petrol to its motorists until the Egyptians had cleared the war debris from the canal and reopened the shipping lanes to the oil refineries. The British Government of Anthony Eden disintegrated and in 1957 power passed to Harold Macmillan, who soon became the great decolonizer of the British Empire in Africa.

The second challenge to British colonial rule in northern Africa came from the Sudan, a colony that was theoretically the joint responsibility of Britain and Egypt but which had in effect been ruled by Britain since Egypt had gained self-government in 1922. In 1948 internal colonial democracy was granted to the Sudan and elected politicians debated whether the country should seek unification with Egypt (whose first republican president had had a Sudanese mother) or whether it should claim full independence. The dominant northern politicians opted for independence on the model chosen by Burma; in 1956 Sudan became a republic and did not join the financial and diplomatic club of former imperial dominions that were becoming a British-led commonwealth of nations. But rapid and total decolonization did not solve the fundamental problem of Sudan's deep division between north and south. The south was racially black in contrast to the north, where a thousand years of Arab immigration had created a light-skinned population, and educated southerners spoke English not Arabic and worshipped in Christian churches rather than Muslim mosques. The two cultural traditions broke into two political traditions that soon came into armed confrontation with each other and the Sudan spasmodically suffered from long periods of civil war. The cultural heritage of empire permeated both sides, bringing to the forefront of politics British-trained officers in the north and Christian converts in the south.

The Second World War had brought a temporary reversal to the long-term trend of British disengagement from northeastern Africa. Both the intensity and the extent of British influence was increased. Indeed, one of the great turning points of the war took place on Egyptian soil when the German Afrika Korps, commanded by Rommel, tried to capture Egypt and open a route to the Middle Eastern oil fields by which to fuel German industry and the German war machine. The drive was halted at El Alamein, outside Alexandria, by a British army commanded by Montgomery. This army brought new prosperity to

13

some Egyptians but also stimulated anti-British sentiments among nationalists and intensified the anti-Western attitudes of Muslims. The latter saw their country being corrupted by soldiers needing to recuperate from desert warfare by patronizing bars and nightclubs staffed by unveiled Egyptian women. In the short term the war not only greatly increased the British presence but also carried British influence beyond its historic sphere in Egypt and Sudan. British soldiers and administrators moved into neighbouring Italian spheres of influence in northeastern Africa and began a process of decolonization in Eritrea on the eastern flank and Libya in the western desert.

Eritrea had become an Italian colony during the "scramble for Africa" and tens of thousands of Italians had settled in the cool highlands above the Red Sea salt deserts. In 1941 the colony was captured by Britain, which imposed a temporary military government until a decision about the colony's future could be settled internationally. Eritreans were politically divided between Christians and Muslims and between those who saw their future as linked to the neighbouring empire of Ethiopia and those who sought independent statehood. In 1950 the United Nations decided that Eritrea should be linked to Ethiopia and a slow process of integration began. At first Eritrea retained democratic institutions and political parties of the type Britain encouraged in its self-governing colonies, but these were gradually wound down as Ethiopian laws replaced Eritrean ones and in 1962 Eritrea was formally absorbed into Ethiopia. Some Eritreans felt betrayed by Britain, which had merely liberated them from Italian rule in order to hand them over to Ethiopian rule. Some of Eritrea's Italian settlers remained during the transition and even prospered under Ethiopian rule. But some Eritrean Christians and many Eritrean Muslims felt that their birthright had been denied them. Gradually, with an eye on decolonizing developments among their southern neighbours in eastern Africa, they began to seek a second independence (see Chapter 3).

The second Italian territory to be decolonized in the immediate aftermath of the Second World War was Libya. After the retreat of the German army, temporary British military rulers were the dominant force controlling both Italian-speaking settlers and Arabic-speaking Libyans. The British favoured the creation of a conservative monarchy that would unite the three regions of Libya and govern them as a single country without any radical upheavals. Their choice of king was Muhammad Idris, the head of the Sanusi religious order, who had returned from exile in Egypt to become the emir of the eastern province of Cyrenaica. In Tripoli, where Italian colonial influence and authority remained strongest, and where nationalist aspirations focused on the creation of a modern industrializing state, the urban population vigorously opposed the British-sponsored agenda for decolonization. By 1951, however, the nationalists acknowledged the United Nations decision that Libya must become independent, and accepted that the best compromise was a federal system in which the province of Tripoli would have some autonomous powers under the overarching government of King Idris. In the nomadic and pastoral south, the province of Fezzan also retained some federal devolution of power. It was from the south that a new Libyan radicalism emerged, which challenged both the religious conservatism of Cyrenaica and the entrepreneurial nationalism of Tripoli. The movement grew up among soldiers who wished to cleanse Libya of its legacy of colonial corruption and adopt a pure form of patriotic and puritanical socialism. Its leader was a visionary colonel, Muammar al-Gaddafi, who aspired to give Libya the most independent government in all Africa. Ironically, he was helped in so doing by the discovery of oil that made Libya the richest country in the African continent.

While Britain was predominantly responsible for taking the initiative in the controlled decolonization of northeastern Africa, France was the main foreign power in northwestern Africa, the region known in Arabic as the Maghreb, "the west". French influence in the Maghreb had grown up in a series of initiatives beginning with the conquest of the capital city Algiers in 1830. It continued with the settlement of European wheat farmers and wine-growers in the Algerian coastlands, and with the conquest of the Algerian hinterland of mountains and deserts. In the 1880s French influence spread eastward with the creation of French Tunisia. Domination of the Maghreb culminated in 1912 with the establishment in the west of a French protectorate over the ancient sultanate of Morocco, a kingdom that, unlike the other territories obtained by France, had proudly maintained its independence since the Middle Ages and never been conquered by the Ottoman empire. The northern and southern provinces of Morocco were partitioned off and given to Spain, which made claims dating back to the age of Columbus.

In 1940, less than 30 years after the annexation of Morocco, France

15

itself was invaded and partitioned. French north Africa came under the influence of the quasi-autonomous regime of Marshal Pétain at Vichy and provided some logistic support to the German and Italian campaigns in Africa. In 1942 British and American forces opposed to Vichy, and nominally sympathetic to the rival French government-in-exile of General Charles de Gaulle, invaded the Maghreb via Morocco and Tunisia and established themselves in Algiers where Harold Macmillan became the British minister resident in north Africa. The Second World War, fought to proclaim the rights of nations to choose their own destinies, not unnaturally led north Africans to believe that they too would benefit from the principles of democracy and self-determination. Initially they were disillusioned. Algerians, who celebrated the end of the European war in May 1945, imagined that independence would now be theirs, but their demands turned into a riotous threat to colonial order; settlers were killed and many demonstrators were shot by white vigilantes, arrested by armed security forces or executed by the colonial law courts. Decolonization in northwestern Africa was delayed by ten years.

The decolonization of Algeria caused a prolonged and destructive confrontation between Europe and Africa, the "savage war of peace", as Macmillan's biographer, Alastair Horne, called it. The prelude to this colonial war, and to the granting of independence, however, took place in the neighbouring territories of Morocco and Tunisia. From the relative safety of Tangier, a Moroccan free port under international control, the sultan of Morocco began subversively to proclaim his country's right to escape from French tutelage and join the independent Arab nations of the Islamic world. At the same time, the Moroccan working class organized strikes demanding better conditions in a country dominated by the economic interests of European settlers and businesses. The conflict increased in intensity, the French deposed the sultan, townsmen boycotted French goods, countrymen took up arms in irregular guerrilla forces, and politicians demanded immediate independence. In 1956 France, having lost one colonial war in Indochina and embarked on another in Algeria, gave way and the sultan returned to become the independent King Mohamed V of Morocco.

On Algeria's eastern flank Tunisia underwent a similar confrontation with France, although the traditional ruler, the Bey of Tunis, did not play a comparable role in ending the protectorate to that achieved by the sultan of Morocco. The nationalist leadership was rooted in an old and well-established urban bourgeoisie whose traditions dated back to the great days of Carthage before the Roman conquest. The Arab politicians had to tread a wary path, listening to the demands of a proletariat whose post-war standard of living was declining, while at the same time negotiating with France over their own middle-class interests. French politicians, on their side, were anxious to avoid the expense of repressing yet another colonial rebellion, but could not ignore the stridency of French settlers in Tunisia anxious to preserve their social and economic privileges. Settler opposition to even gradual political reform blocked the establishment of a Tunisian parliament and led to the arrest of even the most pragmatic of Tunisia's nationalists, Habib Bourguiba. As in Morocco, however, France soon decided to reverse its policy, released the martyred but essentially moderate statesman, conceded internal self-government, and finally granted independence in 1956. Three weeks after the decolonization of Morocco, Bourguiba became president of Tunisia.

The relatively rapid decolonization of all the northern African protectorates, from Morocco to Eritrea, in the ten years following the Second World War, naturally led Algerians to presume that they too could expect to recover responsibility for their own affairs. Algeria, however, was constitutionally very different from any other country in Africa and was administered as though it were three departments of metropolitan France. Formally, relations between France and Algeria resembled relations between Great Britain and Northern Ireland more than those between Europe and Africa. Economically, the situation was very different from other colonial relationships. The scale of French trade and investment in Algeria matched in scale the economic commitments of France in all the other territories of its empire put together. Thus it was that French financiers, and their political associates in Paris, were more reluctant to transfer political power in Algeria than they were in the protectorates or the tropical colonies. Furthermore, the scale of French emigration to Algeria far exceeded the scale of emigration to other French colonies such as Madagascar or Senegal. Indeed, there were almost as many French settlers in Algeria as there were British settlers in South Africa, and the Algerian settlers were almost as strongly attached to their adopted homeland as were the Dutch-speaking Afrikaners in South Africa. The settlers became known as the *pieds-noirs*, the black feet;

17

many were small farmers with their feet rooted in the soil of the black continent. Their lack of alternatives and their fierce peasant determination, like that of the Boer farmers of South Africa, to hold on to what they had won, made it very difficult for the settlers to adapt to changing circumstances. They could not envisage access to new opportunities in the way that the commercial and professional middle classes of many colonies were able to do when seeking profit from changing political circumstances. Thus it was that Algerian nationalists faced a much more difficult task in seeking independence than did Tunisians or Egyptians.

The first formal demand that Algeria should be given independence came not from an educated nationalist elite seeking a political voice inside Algeria, nor even from Algerian Muslims who wanted the restoration of their personal rights and religious dignities, but from the leaders of the 100,000 Algerians who worked in France during the years following the First World War. Their political organizer, Messali Hadj, was a former labourer, army conscript and market barrow-boy who studied classical Arabic and married a French communist. His political agenda was a generation ahead of its time and sought the replacement of the French army of occupation by a national Algerian army; the abolition of the separate legal code that distinguished "natives" from "settlers"; and universal suffrage not only for local government but also in electing a national parliament for an independent Algeria. Like the agenda adopted by Egyptian nationalists 25 years later, it also sought social and economic reforms with security benefits for workers, credit facilities for peasants restored to their lands, the extension of education to the illiterate majority, and the official recognition of Arabic as well as French as a state language. Although these political demands evolved among émigrés in France, who aspired to such socialist measures as the nationalization of banking and industry, the migrant workers did remember their rural roots and asked for irrigation projects and farm roads in the more remote and arid parts of their country. As exploited foreign labour, Algerians in France communicated across the class divisions that so sharply divided Algerians at home. Thus it was that they began to formulate broad ideas and aspirations and blend their nationalism with a popular appeal that filtered back into Algeria itself.

Inside Algeria the nationalist movement was led in the inter-war years by men whose social class differed from that of most migrant workers. The urban elite expected to be assimilated into the privileged class of colonial society in which distinctions would not be based on race, and opportunity would be opened by education, by professional employment and by social integration into the French-speaking community. The programme was slow, however; only a few thousand Algerians had been assimilated to high colonial status and assimilation had barely touched the majority of the middle class by the 1930s. The most far-sighted of the leaders from the middle-class professions, Ferhat Abbas, began to perceive that the fastest way to bring about equality for all Algerians was to seek the transformation of Algeria from a colony into a fully integrated province of France with all the political rights and educational opportunities enjoyed by the French. One powerful French voice, the popular front politician Violette, accepted this line of argument and pointed out that if the prospect of integration were denied to Algerians, nationalist protesters would demand a radical break with France and retaining the colony would become impossible. The settlers vigorously condemned Algerian integration into French society. They forced Paris to denounce assimilation and tried to stem the tide of Algerian aspiration. Severely restricted voting rights were enforced in local elections as well as in electing delegates to the Paris parliament. Abbas and his moderate supporters were eventually forced to turn, as Violette had foreseen, to the alternative option of independence. The triumphant celebrations of the settlers in 1930, at the centenary of their conquest, had by then accelerated Algerian alienation and stimulated the rise of anti-colonial nationalism.

The idealism of Messali Hadj and the pragmatism of Ferhat Abbas were matched by a third strand of Algerian nationalism. This emphasized Arab identity and was problematic since many Algerians were Berbers rather than Arabs and some Muslims, although Arabs, did not support radical nationalist politics. To the settlers, however, Islam and Arabism became symbols of the nationalism that threatened their wellbeing, which depended on the plentiful supply of cheap Arab labourers. Disenchanted Algerians noted that the living standard of whites had risen to seven times that of their Arab contemporaries and neighbours. When in 1936 a Socialist government in Paris tried very cautiously to assuage Algerian frustration and extend the franchise to 20,000 Muslim officers, graduates and civil servants, the anger of the settlers, and Conservative support for them in France, was so strong

19

that the Reform Bill was not even laid before parliament. It was becoming impossible to appease the growing Algerian sense of economic deprivation, the Muslim sense of social inequality and the Arab sense of psychological alienation. In 1944 General de Gaulle, the provisional head of a French government with its capital in Algiers, tried to reopen the political dialogue with the offer of voting rights to 65,000 Europeanized Algerians, but it was still too little and too late. In 1945 rioting broke out and many lives were lost in both communities.

After the Second World War Algeria had some difficulty in creating a unified national identity that appealed to all sections of indigenous society in a campaign for independence. Unlike Morocco, Algeria had no monarchy that could act as a focus for rival factions of nationalist opinion. Unlike Tunisia, it had no old-established and self-confident bourgeoisie that could plan political action in alliance with workers or peasants. The colonial middle class of Algeria was small, insecure in its identity, and found that negotiating compromises among the many interests and factions was made virtually impossible by the settler hostility to open political debate. The continued willingness of the moderate Abbas to attempt to use the democratic process was vitiated by French willingness to collude in the falsifying of election returns. The radical Messali came to believe that only secret subversion of the colonial state would lead to real concessions by France. As Algeria was driven towards war the rival political factions were drawn into the conflict. The first shots were fired on 1 November 1954. All French political opinion rallied to defend the country's richest colony and the Socialist minister of the interior, François Mitterrand, defended the claim that Algeria was part of France. "Who among you", he asked the French people, "would hesitate to use all means to save France?" (cited by Hrbek 1993: 133).

The means used to save French Algeria from the tide of decolonization were brutal. The war methods adopted by both sides came to resemble those seen during the German occupation of France itself ten years earlier. Terrorism was used by some militant Algerians to heighten confrontation when the first year of the war brought little success. Counter-terrorism was the French weapon used to dissuade Algerians from supporting the coalition of nationalist interests that had formed a liberation front. Terror was also used to discourage rural peoples from supplying nationalist units with food and shelter. Where terror was not enough to cut off support for the guerrillas, villagers were uprooted and herded into security hamlets similar to those built by the British to quell a simultaneous rebellion in Kenya. Abroad, the Liberation Front, guided by Ferhat Abbas, gained political support from non-aligned nations and military support from Arab countries, notably Tunisia, which offered an hospitable frontier after 1956. The French response was to seal the frontier with an electric fence reminiscent of the "iron curtain" that divided Europe. But French armed forces, even elite professional regiments and an expeditionary army of nearly half a million conscripts, were not adequate to repress the Algerian rebellion and in 1958 senior army officers demanded more determined government support. The French republic collapsed and special powers were given to General de Gaulle to rule France and end the war.

In 1958 both the white settlers and the colonial financiers were convinced that the old wartime general would bring them a rapid victory. In practice, the interests of Algeria and France had begun to diverge as the war continued with high white casualties, growing political disillusion and, above all, a heavy burden on the exchequer. Moreover, France had now signed the Treaty of Rome and created a European Economic Community that turned some French economic priorities from the Mediterranean in the south to the Rhine basin in the north. De Gaulle realized that the new interests of French industry outweighed the old interests of the colonial settlers. He also realized that the political influence of the families of reluctant conscripts who wanted to abandon the nightmare of colonial war outweighed the aspirations of a professional army that was anxious to win a colonial war to compensate for losing Indochina. The political will to win the war was declining in France and the growing publicity given to the use of torture by the French forces caused widespread revulsion. De Gaulle began to negotiate compromise solutions with Algeria's leaders.

Each attempt at a settlement of the war met with reverses. The Liberation Front's provisional government would not agree to a decolonization that partitioned the country and left the new Saharan oil wells in French political hands rather than merely under French technical and financial control. The settlers were outraged that de Gaulle should even talk to the Algerian provisional government and attempted to organize their own rebellion against France to create a

21

white-ruled republic, but after a week of manning the barricades in Algiers their protest collapsed. A year later the professional soldiers tried to stop the peace process and set up their own secret army of terrorists, which attempted to assassinate de Gaulle. In March 1962 a ceasefire was agreed between the Liberation Front and de Gaulle's peace negotiators. The settler and army response was a wave of sabotage that so alienated Algerians it destroyed any hope that moderate settlers might remain in Africa and help the new republic to find its economic feet. After losing almost one million people in the fighting, Algeria now lost almost another million who emigrated, including the majority of the country's technical experts.

Amidst the stampede of departing settlers the war ended and independence arrived on 5 July 1962. However, decolonization required not only the withdrawal of a colonial power but also its replacement by a recognized national power. Finding a new government for Algeria after the French departure took another three months. Old rivalries between radicals and moderates, between Arabs and Berbers, Muslims and Marxists, civilians and soldiers, and eastern military regions and western military regions, were difficult to resolve among the ruins left by settlers determined to destroy that which they could not take with them. During the war the old leaders, Messali and Abbas, had been gradually eclipsed by new military leaders, the most determined of whom was Houari Boumedienne, a man who transcended some of the factional boundaries. He had had a French education in his home territory in eastern Algeria and had participated in the 1945 riots there, later escaping to Cairo where he gained an Islamic education in Arabic. During the colonial war he rose to command a wing of the Algerian liberation army stationed in Morocco, and then to become chief of staff with greater powers than the nominal president of the provisional government. On the eve of independence the divided politicians tried to recover the civilian initiative and dismiss Boumedienne, while commanders of the home-front units tried to exclude him from sharing the authority they had won in their military districts. Boumedienne fought a virtual civil war to reach Algiers with his political supporters and three years later conducted a *coup d'état* that made him president of the "democratic and popular" republic of Algeria.

By 1962 the largest, richest and most populated of the territories of northern Africa had gained independence. There remained, however, one last footnote to the region's programme of decolonization. This concerned the Spanish colonies along the Atlantic shore of northern Africa. Spain had been an early colonizer, and acquired the Canary Islands from Portugal where the dwindling population of local Berbers was absorbed into a much larger European immigrant population. On the adjacent African mainland Spain acquired colonies in northern Morocco, in southern Morocco and in the Rio de Oro territories of the Western Sahara. Gradually the Spanish claims were whittled away by Moroccan territorial expansion, although the constitutional position of the Western Sahara remained in dispute and two fortress towns in the north remained under Spanish control, eyeing Gibraltar from the African shore of the strait. The offshore Canary Islands, although historically and geographically part of Africa, remained culturally, economically and politically part of Spain.

CHAPTER TWO

Independence and neocolonialism
in western Africa

Western Africa is made up of three parallel bands of grassland, woodland and forest that stretch 2,000 miles from Cape Verde to Mount Cameroun and separate the Sahara desert from the Atlantic beaches. In classical times the region was slightly familiar to Phoenicians, who called it Guinea, "the land of black people"; to Greeks, whose wild adventures of exploration were known to Herodotus; and to Romans, who drove two-wheeled chariots across the desert in search of precious stones. In the Middle Ages western Africa was closely linked to the Muslim Mediterranean by camel caravans, and in the fifteenth century sea links to Christian Europe were pioneered by the Portuguese. For the next three centuries western Africa provided a large part of the labour force required to colonize the Americas, and so many slaves were sold for export that local economic development was sapped and coastal consumers relied on imports rather than fostering domestic industries such as those that grew up in the great inland cities of Kano and Timbuktu. In the nineteenth century the coastal ports became European colonies, each of which carved out a commercial hinterland and often built a railway to facilitate mineral extraction, crop exporting and the rapid transit of soldiers. Apart from the French inland colonies protecting the southern approaches to Algeria, the partition created four French seashore colonies, four British colonies, two Portuguese colonies, one American sphere of influence, and a short-lived German colony that was later shared out between Britain and France. A little over half a century after the partition, around 1960, these colonies were

25

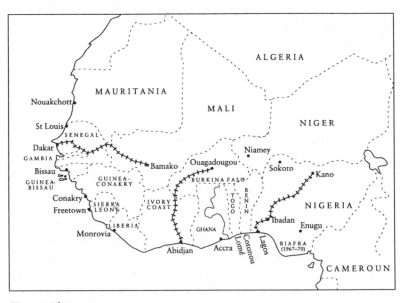

Western Africa

suddenly transformed into 16 independent republics whose ties with Europe were no longer constitutional but cultural and commercial. For better or for worse, colonialism had given way to "neocolonialism".

The roots of anti-colonial nationalism in western Africa date back to the earliest years of imperial domination. The nationalists did not, by and large, belong to the old royal courts and aristocracies that had been either defeated by the colonial invaders or co-opted by them to become their local agents of administration. The new political activists belonged instead to a "modern" generation of men who had been educated in mission schools and government colleges or had gained experience of life beyond the colonial world through travel. Some went abroad in the colonial armies recruited to help Britain and France to fight against Germany in one world war and Japan in the other. Some trained as teachers in France or lawyers in Britain, and a few went as far afield as the United States where they met a black middle class ambitious to overcome the racial inequalities that governed both American and African societies. A handful of worldly Africans admired the visionary Caribbean ideals of Marcus Garvey, who

26

dreamt of creating a pan-African empire in which black peoples would rule their own destinies. In 1945 they met in a pan-African congress under the American chairmanship of W. E. B. Dubois and discussed their hopes of a post-war world in which fragmented Africa would be decolonized and united as a proud black nation. The first step had to be the winning of independence. The pioneer of decolonization in western Africa was to be Ghana's Kwame Nkrumah, who had acted as an organizing secretary to the 1945 congress.

Colonial Ghana, the Gold Coast, enjoyed many advantages in the colonial world. It was moderately prosperous with a level of wealth that almost attained that of some non-industrial countries in Mediterranean Europe. It had a network of schools whose English-speaking pupils could staff clerical posts in both government and business. It had a small but rising population of university graduates who provided decision-making skills at a level more commonly found in northern and southern Africa than in the territories of tropical Africa. The black middle class had won responsibility in city politics and even gained seats on the judicial bench and in the legislative council of the colony. The professional men were supported by a few African businessmen who cautiously put a little of their money into organizing a political party called the United Gold Coast Convention. The party decided to hire an organizing secretary to run errands, convene meetings, keep minutes, and staff an office rented from a colonial trading store. Their choice fell on Nkrumah, a Catholic-trained schoolmaster who had spent ten years studying theology, philosophy and politics in the United States and gained some experience as a student organizer in post-war Britain. The choice was inspired; although Nkrumah did not prove to be an ideal employee, he was a tireless campaigner and a brilliant speaker. His radical political agenda ran far ahead of the men who had appointed him and he demanded immediate freedom from colonial rule and justice with equality for all. The colonial authority considered his fiery oratory and seditious journalism to be subversive and arrested him on more than one occasion. In the short breathing space that it gained while Nkrumah was in gaol the British Government was forced to make a choice between repression and liberation as its strategy. It chose liberation.

The British decision to initiate a policy of decolonization in Ghana was not intended to unravel the whole British empire, let alone to trigger off independence movements in all the other empires in Africa. It was a decision taken with regard to local circumstance in a specific case. Decolonization in Ghana was thought to be reasonably safe. There were no white settlers whose racial privileges needed special protection. The production of cocoa, the major source of wealth, was in the hands of African farmers who could be expected to continue to trade with Britain. The gold mines were British-owned, and anticipated no threats to continuity that skilled management and responsible trade unions could not handle. The working relationship between African civil servants and expatriate ones was excellent and administrative stability and continuity could be expected. The only question mark lay over the choice of politicians who would be elected to the colonial parliament as the stages of self-government were introduced. A wise and experienced new governor, Sir Charles Arden-Clarke, would have preferred not to have to deal with Nkrumah whom he slightingly described as "aping Hitler" (Rooney 1982: 91). But when, in black Africa's first general election, Nkrumah successfully inspired the electorate from prison and won a convincing parliamentary majority for his people's party, the governor recommended that he be appointed leader of government business. The two men developed a close working relationship and the governor soon upgraded Nkrumah's appointment to that of prime minister.

In the phrase of the time Ghana was thought to be "ready for independence" in a way that other colonies were not, at least not in the eyes of Europeans who wanted to keep a tight control over the course of events. But Ghana had set an agenda that all Africa was listening to on wirelesses that could pick up news of the "African revolution" from stations as far away as Cairo, beyond the reach of colonial censorship. The course of decolonization had been conceded rather than directed by Britain. The speed of change was determined not by the lawyers of the old Gold Coast convention who had set the movement in train, but by young school-leavers with unlimited ambition and self-confidence. Decolonization was driven by market women with no training in "readiness for independence" but with immense experience in the management of retail business, and by wage-workers and war-pensioners who understood that their earnings were slipping backwards in a foreign-run economy. Some Ghana politicians tried to slow the tempo, change the political emphasis, favour regional interests, restore power to the aristocracy, but the slogans "one man, one vote" and "freedom now" were too powerful to be curbed. Nkrumah won his third general election in 1956 and Ghana was granted independence in 1957.

A later generation of African politicians learnt that after independence "the struggle goes on". In 1957 this slogan was not yet current and the politicians who won victory with the appeal of decolonization were astonished to discover how difficult and expensive it would be to implement the rest of their agenda for social change in a postcolonial age. Democracy involved reconciling opposing policies and making difficult choices without causing offence that threatened order and stability. Colonial governments had been relatively dictatorial and provided little experience for settling differences of political priority in the public arena. But new governments had not only to learn the art of domestic politics, they also had to learn to deal with foreign affairs. In the case of Ghana the political priority was industrialization. The nearest models available were those of the United States and the Soviet Union, which only 20 years earlier had pioneered frontiers of development and created new wealth with programmes of industrialization based on hydroelectric energy rather than coal. Ghana, like Egypt, therefore put a high priority on seeking foreign capital to dam its local river and create the world's largest hydroelectric lake. In so doing the government discovered just how little international influence a small decolonized nation could wield and how strong were the financial and engineering forces controlled by the "neocolonial" powers. Ghana built its dam, but the price it had to pay for both the finance and the engineering was too high and profits were long postponed. Worse still, Ghana's ambition to build an integrated aluminium industry to quarry and smelt local bauxite and then process and sell finished aluminium goods was ruled out by the contractors. They only wanted cheap power to turn their own semi-processed aluminium into refined bars in a way that would bring minimum cost and maximum profit to North American industries and offered the leanest possible margin for Africa. Nkrumah became more convinced than ever that successful decolonization required close co-operation between African neighbours if international bargaining was to be beneficial to Africa.

Ghana was unusual in that after independence its president retained a strong commitment to the old ideals of pan-Africanism and appeared willing to court great unpopularity by neglecting nationalist ambition at home and favouring transnational co-operation. The first conference of independent African states brought together seven very disparate polities: the two Arab kingdoms of Morocco and Libya, the empire of Ethiopia and the Creole republic of Liberia (both clients of the United States), the radical republic of Egypt and the conservative republic of Tunisia, with the commonwealth dominion of Ghana acting as host. The seven leaders had few common objectives and so Nkrumah next summoned a conference of "African peoples" attended by politicians from colonies that were not yet free and whose leaders were inspired by a personal visit to Ghana, the showcase of decolonization. Five years later, when many of these politicians met again in Ethiopia, the map of Africa had been transformed and a majority of them had won independence. The idea of surrendering power to a pan-African ideal no longer excited them, however, and their agendas were parochially nationalist. The new presidents protected as sovereign frontiers the boundaries that had been so arbitrarily laid down by the Victorian colonizers, and the Organization of African Unity they founded had only the most limited power or prestige. In 1965 Nkrumah made one last bid to establish the nucleus of a pan-African government, but his fellow leaders snubbed him and his own people became disenchanted with his expensive ideals. A few months later, days after unveiling his great dam, Nkrumah was swept away. Among those dissatisfied with his policies were members of both the police force and the army. The police had been infiltrated by corruption and feared an investigation of its practices, while the army felt threatened by new Russian military traditions that challenged the prestige of its old British customs. Together they seized power and Africa lost its apostle of unity.

One subtle, immediate, and effective challenge to the pan-African ideal of postcolonial co-operation came from France. After the Second World War French policy in western Africa tended towards the object of assimilating African leaders into European culture, drawing the colonial territories together in a federal government based on the great commercial and strategic harbour of Dakar, and linking Africa ever more closely to France by providing it with a few elected seats in the French parliament and appointing token African politicians to posts in the French Government. This policy was undermined by the British decision, made by a Labour Government in 1951 but soon endorsed by Conservatives, to devolve power to its colonies in western Africa. French policy switched from integration to "Balkanization" – the dividing of the empire into small autonomous units as practised in the nineteenth-century decolonization of the Balkan states of the Turkish empire in eastern Europe. When in 1958 de Gaulle was given special powers in Paris to resolve the Algerian war, he realized that the decolonization of tropical Africa needed to be a part of his grand design. He visited Africa dangling a carrot and wielding a stick. The carrot was the offer of special privileges to colonial politicians, funds for economic and educational development, and free access to Paris society where elite Africans felt culturally at home. The price was the acceptance of membership of a French union that would be much more closely knit than the British commonwealth and in which France would make the grand strategic decisions. The stick was short and blunt: any colony that voted *Non* to de Gaulle's union would be cast out to fend for itself without access to the technical, financial or philosophical comforts. All but one of France's tropical African colonies accepted de Gaulle's limited form of semi-independence in 1958.

De Gaulle's blueprint for French decolonization, and the creation of numerous small states that would each be individually tied to Paris, was a defiant challenge to the ideal of pan-African integration and even to the more localized prospect of a United States of West Africa that could negotiate with European powers on more equitable terms. For a moment it seemed that de Gaulle's gamble might not pay off. One territory, Guinea, did not vote *Oui* in the referendum. Its leaders had not emerged from the assimilated Francophile elite but from a trade-union movement that had much less cause to be beholden to France. They mounted a vigorous referendum campaign and Guinea voted for total independence and against the French union. De Gaulle carried out his threat and withdrew not only administrative and technical personnel but also material equipment such as vehicles and telephones in the hope that he could make an independent Guinea ungovernable. The pan-Africanists counter-attacked by giving Guinea diplomatic and financial assistance and sponsoring its admission to the United Nations as the second decolonized member from black Africa. De Gaulle was forced rapidly to improve the terms that he had offered to his loyal colonial followers. In 1960 they too were given a form of independence that entitled them to a seat at the United Nations. The new terms, however, flattered the vanity of the politicians and used the patriotic discourse of nationalism while preserving in French hands the realities of military and financial power.

De Gaulle achieved his decolonizing objectives at the second attempt and the eight former colonies each followed their own distinct path of postcolonial politics. The people of Benin, who had been known for their educational achievements and had provided trained staff for other parts of French Africa, found their opportunities in an autonomous micro-state very restricted and experimented with semi-communist paths out of their relative poverty. In the Benin hinterland the territory of Niger was nominally decolonized but remained effectively under French military control. The Ivory Coast, which had been largely neglected in colonial times and whose leaders had been particularly reluctant to accept independence rather than pursue integration with France, adopted a policy of attracting colonial-style settlers to create wealth. White entrepreneurs driven out of French Vietnam helped establish a vibrant plantation economy, and Arab immigrants from the former French territory of Lebanon created a countrywide network of rural transport, village shops and peasant credit facilities. These Lebanese shrewdly won support from their customers, and protection from greedy nationalist politicians, by sponsoring and funding local football teams. African soccer became one of the visible symbols of continental co-operation, although the best African players often gravitated to employment with Marseille and other affluent European teams. The northern hinterland of the Ivory Coast, at the end of the colonial railway, became first a separate colony and later the republic of Burkina Faso. It was briefly led by an inspired young officer, Thomas Sankara, before reverting to a conventional pattern of peasant poverty and neocolonial subservience.

Senegal had Africa's oldest links with France and faced the hardest task of postcolonial adaptation. Four old French communes, including the city of Saint Louis on the edge of the great Mauritanian desert, were gradually incorporated into Senegal during the course of the twentieth century. Their populations of black French citizens surrendered the social status and political rights that they had acquired over the previous three centuries to the largely Muslim and rural peoples of the hinterland. The dialogue between the French urban tradition of "assimilated citizens" and the rural one of "associated subjects" was skilfully orchestrated by the 1960s generation of politicians who came from the countryside but spoke the language of the city. The first difficulty of decolonization arose when the city of Dakar lost its administrative role as the capital of the disbanded federation of French western Africa and the elite had to seek new outlets for their talent and training. The great harbour also lost its commercial primacy. The Senegal politicians tried to maintain a political hold on part of their hinterland but the leaders of Mali rebelled, cut the railway line, and even threatened to join forces with the recalcitrant republic of Guinea. One political and economic oddity of Senegal was that the region's only navigable river, the Gambia, had fallen to the British during the Anglo-French wars of the slaving era, and although Senegal tried to claim it, both during the colonial partition and after decolonization, it remained an autonomous English-speaking enclave visited by British tourists in times of peace but occasionally patrolled by French-speaking Senegalese gendarmes in times of tension. Senegal's leaders remained steadfastly loyal to France and were rewarded, but Senegalese peasants continued to export unprocessed peanuts and Senegalese workers continued to eat French bread for which they paid dearly. Any sign of protest could be quelled by the small French military force that remained to monitor the behaviour of the decolonized client republic. Senegal's president, the poet Léopold Senghor, retained his country seat in Normandy, wrote about *négritude*, the pride of being black, and was elected to the Académie Française.

In 1960 the fragmentation of French western Africa had presented one challenge to the ideals of pan-Africanism. In the same year a quite different challenge came from the decolonization and consolidation of Nigeria, the African giant that occupied the eastern portion of western Africa. Nigeria was so large that it did not need pan-African integration, and so complex that all its political energies were absorbed inwards. Although Nigeria only covered about three per cent of Africa's land surface, it contained almost a quarter of its population. The population was large and growing, and it was also very diverse; governing it proved difficult not only for the colonizing British administrators of 1900, but also for the decolonizing Nigerian politicians of 1960. The British had solved their problem in two ways. In the south they had encouraged the spread of Christian education and created an English-speaking network of Yoruba people in the west and Igbo people in the east who acted as intermediaries between the vibrant local cultures and the foreign economic interests. In the north a quite different solution allowed Islam to retain its supremacy and granted the Hausa emirs of the fallen sultanate of Sokoto the right to rule their kingdoms on behalf of Britain. British

33

overlordship in Nigeria was exercised by three sets of officials: one east, one west and one north, each directly or indirectly responsible for order, for revenue, and for the free flow of palm oil, cocoa and peanuts along the colonial roads and railways that superseded the old caravan footpaths.

The search for a postcolonial political structure that would protect British economic interests while satisfying the ambitions of rival politicians proved much more difficult in Nigeria than it had in Ghana. Not the least of the controversies concerned how many seats to give to each of the three regions in a central parliament when no one had been able to conduct a population census that was accepted by all as free and fair. Eventually a compromise was achieved that gave considerable powers to the prime ministers of the three regions and somewhat limited power to a federal government. This initial compromise, however, did not last long and the decolonization of Nigeria involved a ten-year process of trial and error. The first federal government was a coalition of north and east, which caused political disruption in the west where politicians rightly felt that they had lost access to the power of political patronage and the awarding of government contracts. The second federal government was a coalition of the northern emirs and some factions of the western establishment, but this caused rival westerners, and all easterners, to feel that they had been deprived of a political voice. The third central government was a military one that aimed to restore southern influence but also to swing patronage away from civilians and into the hands of soldiers. The fourth was brought about by a northern counter-coup and in 1967 Nigeria broke into civil war.

The Nigerian civil war showed not only how difficult the reconciling of political differences was in countries where the colonizers had introduced no democratic tradition, but also how determined the former colonial powers were to retain or expand their spheres of influence. Although the war was civil, it attracted more or less discreet interventions from both Britain and France who backed rival military factions in the hope of winning long-term strategic benefits. The immediate cause of the war was the declining wellbeing of the east. Although the Igbo had not held political power at the centre for long, they had long enjoyed rich economic opportunities by migrating to the north, and to a lesser extent to the west, and finding employment both as private artisans, merchants and entrepreneurs and also as salaried clerks, bookkeepers and government officials. Their success, and particularly perhaps their success as moneylenders, made them unpopular immigrants and their rights and opportunities as fellow Nigerians were vigorously challenged outside their home region. In 1966 Igbo immigrants in the north were attacked and killed by jealous Hausa neighbours much as Jews had been attacked in many parts of Europe a few years earlier. Thousands packed their belongings to return home, but eastern Nigeria, already more crowded than any other part of Nigeria, had no salaried jobs for returnees, and was short of farmland even for those who were willing to return to peasant subsistence after becoming accustomed to consumer comfort. The despair of the Igbo refugees provided an opening for a disappointed Igbo colonel, Ojukwu, who had been passed over for promotion in the federal army. He returned home and told the Igbo that they could not trust their fellow Nigerians and should seek their own destiny as the independent republic of Biafra.

The secession of Biafra from Nigeria was an important chapter in the history of decolonization. First, it split the Organization of African Unity, whose members had hitherto defended the territorial integrity of former colonies. Some member-states now felt that the atrocities committed against the Igbo justified their claim to a breakaway independence. Secondly, the secession highlighted the growing importance of oil politics in Africa. The new government of Biafra hoped that it could gain economic viability by selling its petroleum directly to the world market without sharing its mineral royalties with less well-endowed regions of Nigeria. Thirdly, the break demonstrated how difficult the politics of partition could be when Biafra found that some of its claimed citizens were hostile to being incorporated into an Igbo-dominated state. On the other hand, Biafra was not satisfied with the limits of the old provincial border either and tried to expand its territory to include oil wells just beyond its reach. Fourthly, the rebellion showed just how urgently France wanted to extend its influence in Africa and more especially to gain access to territory rich in petroleum. While France, and also Portugal, covertly supported the secession, Britain, and also the Soviet Union, supported the federal government, each anticipating long-term benefits from its short-term military assistance to the protagonists. Fifthly and finally, the Biafran war dramatically enhanced humanitarian concern for Africa and generated liberal hostility to neocolonial interventions that brought about mass starvation. American President Lyndon Johnson deliberately provoked an immediate response to Biafra when he ordered his foreign policy team to "get those nigger babies off my TV set" before liberal revulsion could damage his policies (Morris 1977: 42). The world recognized that decolonization was not simply the handing of fancy constitutions made in Westminster to political elites trained at the London Inns of Court, but involved a complex and potentially slow learning of the political art of compromise and concession. In Nigeria the compromises and concessions necessary for peace and unity were made in 1970, but the politicians who made them were trained in Britain's Royal Military Academy and they profitably kept power in the hands of officers for most of the next 30 years.

In westernmost Africa colonies with a much longer experience of colonial rule than Nigeria faced conflict of a rather different kind from that experienced in Biafra. Several islands and enclaves along the northern coast of Guinea were inhabited by black communities of Creole peoples whose social customs had been borrowed from Europe in the nineteenth century. Their leaders spoke pidgin English in Sierra Leone, black American in Liberia and Creole Portuguese in Guinea-Bissau. They did not always communicate well with their rural neighbours who spoke numerous vernaculars and viewed the colonial experience with particular dismay. The Creole population of Sierra Leone had black ancestors who had been brought from eighteenth-century North America after the war of independence, and from nineteenth-century Nigeria when victims of the slave trade were rescued from ships on the high sea and brought to "Freetown" to build a new life under the loose governance of Britain and the moral authority of Christian missions. The descendants of the most successful black settlers were businessmen, journalists, army officers and medical practitioners, who sent their children to west Africa's first university college and tried to uphold the assimilationist tradition of the British empire against the twentieth-century rise of racism. When the clamour for decolonization in western Africa became irresistible after 1960, Britain could not transfer power to the elitist descendants of old settlers – even black settlers – and Freetown had to share power with politicians elected from the provinces. An adequate political culture did not take root, however, and a military tradition of dictatorship gradually developed to eclipse both the country politicians and the city Creoles.

In Liberia political realities followed a similar path to those of Sierra Leone, although constitutional history was rather different. In the early nineteenth century the black settlers and their Christian pastors were planted by the United States on a sparsely peopled stretch of coast and within a generation were given "independence" to conduct their own affairs and defend themselves against their African neighbours. In the twentieth century the Creolized settlers mortgaged their land to an American company that recruited "native" labour to work on its rubber plantations. The rising new market for motor tyres helped to finance the privileged wellbeing of the Creole bourgeoisie in an embryonic city. The Creoles elected their own president every four years, after the American example, and believed themselves to be independent. To the indigenous Liberians, however, the country was effectively a colony, belonging to the American dollar zone and administered by an oligarchy of foreign origin. After 1945 slow transformations occurred that matched those of other west African countries, the economy was diversified, politics spread to include the people of the hinterland, but the change was so slow that impatient young soldiers were permitted to seize control in the 1980s and, as in Sierra Leone, brought about destruction rather than reform.

The oldest Creole community in western Africa in the 1960s was in Guinea-Bissau. Five centuries earlier Portuguese sea merchants had created cotton and sugar plantations on the uninhabited offshore islands of Cape Verde. Ties of commerce and migration grew between the islands and the mainland, and merchant families with large networks of relatives and clients became the basis of Portugal's colonial claims to the Guinea coast during the scramble for Africa. When, a century late, other colonizers began to transfer power to local politicians in Senegal and Sierra Leone, Portugal refused to follow the same path and in 1963 an armed rebellion broke out in Guinea-Bissau. The leader of the rebellion was an agricultural development officer called Amilcar Cabral, who belonged to the Cape Verde elite but whose ideology was directed towards the liberation of colonial peasants. With some help and ideological sympathy from neighbouring Guinea-Conakry, whose radical leaders had rejected the French programme of decolonization offered by de Gaulle, Cabral organized a guerrilla army among the largely Muslim subject peoples of the interior. For ten years the fighting men held at bay a much larger and better equipped colonial army sent to reconquer the territory and resist the English and French principle of transferring power to approved African political partners. After ten years, and despite a plot fomented in the guerrilla army in 1973 in which Cabral was assassinated, the Portuguese failed and their commander, General António Spínola, declared that the colonial reconquest of Guinea-Bissau was impossible. He recommended that negotiation with the guerrillas and the search for a decolonized Portuguese commonwealth or union was the only alternative to an everlasting struggle.

Spínola's political agenda, published in 1973 as "Portugal and the future", had an unexpected impact on the decolonization of Africa. First of all, it gave the Portuguese army a moral licence to refuse to fight any further colonial wars. Young professional soldiers mounted a military *coup d'état* in Lisbon, which brought down an authoritarian regime that had ruled for 48 years and whose credibility had been heavily dependent on preserving the empire. Soon afterwards the Creole population of the Cape Verde islands won its independence and, through its close links with Guinea-Bissau, the ruling party on the islands became the ruling party on the mainland as well. To many people in Guinea-Bissau independence had only been half won as long as the island Creoles retained their influence and a military uprising brought a shift in power from islanders to mainlanders that completed the political decolonization. It failed, however, to bring about the ideals that had made Cabral one of the foremost political thinkers of the African revolution. Nevertheless, his intellectual legacy of an idealized society in which peasants were given full rights and opportunities continued to inspire politicians beyond the confines of western Africa, most notably in Tanzania in eastern Africa.

CHAPTER THREE

Armed struggle and liberation in eastern Africa

Eastern Africa stretches from the coral reefs of the Indian Ocean westward to the great lakes of the upper Nile and northward to the Somali deserts of the Red Sea. It consists of four large countries, each with more than 20 million people, and a dozen smaller ones, half of which are island states in the Indian Ocean. These island states were mostly colonized by France, at one time or another, and retained a degree of French culture even when they were taken over by Britain during the Napoleonic wars. The small mainland states variously experienced colonial rule by Germany, Belgium, Italy and France during the twentieth century and were among the countries of Africa that later had the greatest difficulty in finding stable government. Notable tragedies occurred in formerly Italian Somalia and formerly Belgian Rwanda. At the end of the Second World War the four large countries were all under British domination, although the nature of that domination differed in each case. Uganda, on the fertile upper banks of the Nile, was a protectorate, many of whose people were still loyal to their indigenous kings although subservient to Britain. Kenya, which contained some lush highland surrounded by dry thorn bush, was administratively a true colony and had a small community of white settlers who played a significant role in the history of decolonization. Tanzania, the great hill-ringed plateau of the south, was a colonial mandate, governed by Britain on behalf of the United Nations, which had taken over the supervision of colonies confiscated from Germany at the end of the First World War. And finally, Ethiopia, the ancient mountain empire of the north, was under emergency military rule,

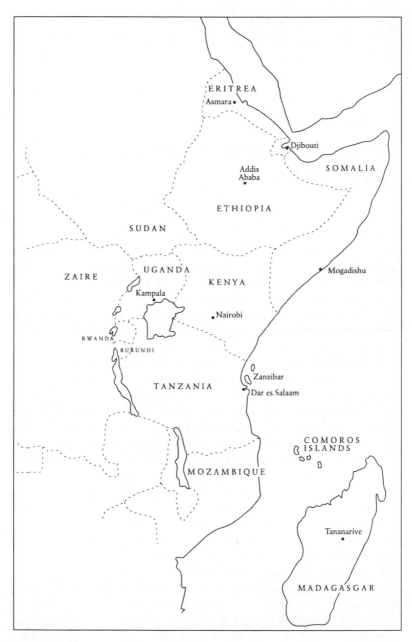

ERITREA
Asmara ●

Djibouti

SOMALIA

Addis
Ababa
●

ETHIOPIA

SUDAN

ZAIRE

UGANDA

Kampala ●

KENYA

Mogadishu ●

● Nairobi

RWANDA

BURUNDI

Zanzibar

Dar es Salaam ●

TANZANIA

COMOROS
ISLANDS

MOZAMBIQUE

MADAGASGAR

Tananarive
●

Eastern Africa

having been conquered by Britain to end seven years of Italian occupation. Ethiopia was the country that made the first east African bid for a return to sovereign independence.

When the British invaded Ethiopia they brought with them Haile Selassie, the prince and war-lord who had become regent of the empire in 1916, been crowned emperor in 1930, and had then been driven into exile in 1935 when the European armies of Mussolini invaded his country from the adjacent Italian colonies of Eritrea and Somalia. Once the Italians had been expelled the British military administration was slow to restore full powers to the emperor, fearing perhaps a colonial vacuum that might be filled to its strategic disadvantage. Britain may also have been reluctant to face the precedent of granting full powers to a black head of state. The emperor may have been declared "free and independent", but Britain effectively controlled his police force, his judiciary, his diplomatic corps and his exchequer. Over the next ten years British influence gradually waned as American influence grew. America particularly wanted to establish a strategic base for surveillance in the Middle East. The ideal location for such a post in the days before satellites was in the northern highlands of the Horn of Africa. America therefore persuaded Britain to surrender the administration of the old Italian colony of Eritrea to the now restored empire of Ethiopia. The United States thereafter increased its stake in Ethiopia and expanded its health and agriculture programme to include military support for the emperor. The policy was not disinterested. In 1952 the revolution in Egypt had brought unwelcome change to Africa and conservative royal governments were no longer seen as wholly dependable allies of Western interests but rather as needing strategic support. The military alliance between the United States and Ethiopia was designed to protect the region from nationalist or socialist aspirations that America considered undesirable rather than to uphold a proud and ancient empire. In the long run, however, American policy failed to protect the aristocracy or to preserve the post-war settlement.

The crises of Ethiopia that led to war with Somalia, the fall of the emperor, the departure of the Americans, the creation of a military dictatorship, the signing of a treaty with the Soviet Union, and the loss of Eritrea, all had their roots in Britain's piecemeal decolonization of the Horn of Africa. The central and most lasting issue was the question of Eritrea, which, having been taken from Italy and given to Ethiopia in 1952, now sought a "second decolonization". Although many Eritreans, especially but not exclusively Christians, had favoured the federal link with Ethiopia, many Muslims had wanted independence. They rightly feared that the postcolonial institutions of parliamentary democracy installed by Britain in Eritrea would not be protected. Gradually the laws of Ethiopia, and despotic rule by imperial decree, were extended to Eritrea and in 1962 the federation was abolished and Eritrea was absorbed into the empire without significant foreign protest. Eritrean nationalists went into exile and prepared to mount a long war of liberation that so undermined the politics of Ethiopia it became one cause of the fall of the empire and the creation of an Ethiopian military dictatorship. The new army regime tried to hold Eritrea for another 20 years, now with Soviet rather than American support, but had no more success than the emperor had achieved, and in 1994 the second independence of Eritrea was recognized.

If Eritrea provided the crises that proved fatal to both the imperial and the military governments of Ethiopia, the three neighbouring Somali colonies were almost equally uncomfortable neighbours. The northern French section of the Somali territory controlled the port at the end of Ethiopia's commercial and strategic railway and continued to do so, despite nominal decolonization, when it became a military base for the French foreign legion. The central British section of the Somali nation laid post-war claims to swathes of inland grazing behind their arid coast, but in the 1950s this land was granted to Ethiopia, leaving Somali nationalists bitterly anxious for revenge. The southern Italian section of Somalia was treated in equally cavalier fashion. In defiance of Somali nationalist feelings the Western powers persuaded the United Nations to hand Somalia back to Italy, although with the proviso that the Italians should prepare the territory for independence within ten years. The decision was a blow to those who sought immediate independence, but it was also a slow fuse for nationalists elsewhere who began to see 1960 as a target date for the decolonization of black Africa. When 1960 arrived the British and Italian zones agreed to form a joint republic. The new nation aspired to recover and unify all the lands of "greater Somalia" and won some support for the project from the Soviet Union in exchange for the granting of military and naval facilities on the Indian Ocean. But the attempts to expand Somalia failed, the Soviet Union shifted its alliance to Ethiopia, and the republic fell apart as the rival clans fought one another for access to scarce land, water and foreign patronage. The United States took over the military and naval leases but was unable to restore a semblance of statehood to Africa's most fragmented former colony.

To the south of Somalia the decolonization of Kenya was one of the classic cases of African decolonization. Although Kenya was the last major country in eastern Africa to gain independence, its armed struggle played a pioneering role in the region in the same way that Ghana's constitutional struggle led the way in western Africa. The conflict over Kenyan independence somewhat resembled the conflict over independence in Algeria, although the white settler population in Kenya was barely a tenth of the size of the settler population in Algeria. Although Kenya became a prized British colony worth defending by force of arms, its origins were almost accidental. Late Victorian Britain wanted to control the headwaters of the Nile, and in order to get there had to cross a thousand miles of sparsely peopled east African savanna, through which they eventually built a railway. Along the route they passed two small areas of fertile, well-farmed highland, from which they decided to extract cash crops that could be carried by rail and so subsidize the running costs of their strategic iron road. The railway workshops at Nairobi became a market town and a few hundred white immigrants bought up plots in the highlands to grow coffee and wheat. Their success was so limited that they were unable to recruit labourers by offering an attractive wage. Instead they persuaded the colonial administration to coerce neighbouring Africans into working for them either by imposing taxes in colonial money that had to be earned on foreign farms or, even more harshly, by expelling Africans from their lands so that they could no longer survive as independent farmers and were forced to work on the colonial estates. In Kenya the injury of this colonial economic policy was not adequately mitigated, as in other colonies, by new opportunities for Africans in salaried service, or in commercial and industrial enterprise. Instead the colonizers brought to the highlands an Asian middle class that had long been active in the towns and harbours of the Kenyan coast and on the Asian-ruled island sultanate of Zanzibar. This colonial system survived the world depression of the 1930s, revived during the war in the 1940s, but was challenged by the African awakening of the 1950s.

The received idea that colonies were run by administrations that

43

were the direct agents of metropolitan economic interests concerned to drain away the raw wealth of Africa was too simple to fit Kenya. There the authorities constantly had to decide whether to support white settlers against black workers or whether the encouragement of black farming might not be in the best interest of Britain. Despite the preferences given to white landowners and to the Asian middle class, some Kenyans found ways to survive in the colonial era and even to profit from the opportunities it presented. Far from all being undifferentiated black peasants and migrants struggling to survive at the bottom of the economic heap, some colonial subjects became very adept at straddling the divides of opportunity between a subsistence economy and the colonial economy. Wages earned as herdsmen on white dairy farms, as woodmen on company plantations, as errand boys for the administration, or as porters for Asian businesses, were invested in the family farms of the homelands that the colonizers had staked out as "labour reserves" bordering their white highlands. Even more successful were the migrant farmers who left the reserves to work on settler estates as "squatters" and gained permission for families to live on spare white land where they reared their own livestock and planted their own crops for domestic consumption and for the market. The roots of the Kenyan revolution, as of so many other revolutions, have to be sought in frustrated success rather than in persistent poverty. The Kenyans who felt most frustrated in the early 1950s were Kikuyu speakers whose tentacles of opportunity spread from their highland homes to the white farms of the Rift Valley and to urban job-seeking in Nairobi.

The Mau Mau rebellion that culminated in the decolonization of Kenya began in 1952 when subversive groups of disenchanted Africans came together and secretly swore to co-operate no longer with colonial authority. Some of them were Kikuyu labourers and squatters on the Rift Valley estates whose livelihood was threatened by changes in colonial farming, by the advent of labour-saving machinery, by the ending of the wartime commodity boom, and by the white recruitment of cheaper, non-Kikuyu labour that displaced them and ended their years of relative prosperity. Some of the rebels were peasants in the reserves who resented increased crowding on African land where they had to support families on dwindling plots. They also resented the chiefs who had been compelled, or induced, to become the agents of colonial rule, levying taxes and conscripting labour.

Most of all, they objected to the interference of colonial "experts" who insisted that they devote hard labour to the unproductive, although well-intentioned, digging of anti-erosion terraces. The rebellion also recruited followers in the city, not among the tiny salaried elite who supported a black cultural and political organization called the Kenya African Union, but among young, angry, underemployed Kikuyu who had escaped from the poverty of farming in the belief that the wooden sidewalks of Nairobi's muddy streets might be paved with gold.

The rebellion brought lasting change to the Kenyan state in general and to Kikuyu society in particular. Several settler families were killed, thus putting the white population on a war footing and driving the rebels to seek refuge in the deepest forest or, initially, in the city slums. The British brought in an army of conscripts from Europe and recruited an African "home guard" of Kenyans compelled to fight against their kith and kin. The death toll in the war was borne mainly by Kikuyu, killed either as suspected terrorists or for collaborating with the colonial enemy. Thousands of small farmers were put in detention camps as "hard core" rebels or rounded up into security hamlets as potential sympathizers. As the emergency was brought to an end these farmers were gradually released, given consolidated plots of land, and encouraged to become small businessmen growing coffee, vegetables and rice for the market. As decolonization approached the more successful of the new black farmers were offered plots on land bought from white settlers by the colonial state. But land distribution did not end with the creation of a class of small capitalist peasants. Very rapidly the entrepreneurial talent of Kenyans, hitherto restricted by colonial and racial preferences, was unleashed, and new black landowners came to eclipse the old white settlers. Family peasants, who had expected independence to restore land and opportunity to them, were sorely disappointed. The Mau Mau "land and freedom army" gained little, but the new entrepreneurs were rewarded not only economically but also by being granted political power.

The most successful power-broker in Kenya was Jomo Kenyatta, a minor Kikuyu official who had gone to Britain in the 1930s, studied anthropology, survived the Second World War in exile, visited the Soviet Union, and returned to Kenya as a political activist. When the rebellion broke out the British arrested him, although he had no knowledge of Mau Mau or influence over it, and he become a symbol of freedom while detained in a desert outpost of the northern frontier. He emerged in 1961 to bring Kenya's conflicting political interests together. He charmed the white farmers, formed a coalition with radical leaders from the western province, absorbed into his party the Kikuyu who had worked for the colonial administration, and finally won an election that enabled him to claim independence. The opposition to his consensus was regional and ethnic rather than ideological. But in winning independence Kenyatta incurred large political debts that had to be repaid. Opportunities for wealth creation and salaried public service were given to the most powerful of the Kikuyu clans while land-hungry peasants who had borne the brunt of the liberation struggle were neglected. As power became concentrated in the centre of the country politicians from the western provinces were marginalized to become a radical opposition that was gradually suppressed. Kenya moved towards presidential rule with, in effect, a single political party. Those associated with that party prospered but many others did not, as peasant holdings shrank to ever smaller units and as the slums of Nairobi mushroomed with an exploding birthrate and an influx of job seekers driven from the land. The state had been decolonized, but in order to hold it together the colonial apparatus of security forces and political repression had to be retained. When Kenyatta died in 1978 the privileged power-base shifted from the Kikuyu of the eastern side of the formerly white Rift Valley to the Kalenjin of the western side of the valley, but the polarization of wealth in postcolonial society continued much as before.

The decolonization of Uganda, Kenya's western neighbour, presented political problems of a different kind from those encountered in a white settler colony. But rivalries of social class and ethnic culture nonetheless frustrated the nationalist dialogue with Britain over the terms of political evolution. Although Uganda had no white settlers it did have an influential community of Asian settlers that the British had brought in to act as middlemen between peasants who grew cotton and companies that exported it. Cotton was never one of Africa's most profitable exports and the farmers were very sensitive both to reductions in crop revenue and inflation in consumer prices in Asian village stores after the Second World War. Immediate blame could be placed on the traders, but as national awareness grew Ugandans accused Britain of holding them in colonial bondage and sought leaders who might protect their interests. One prospective leader who caused the British anxiety was Mutesa, the young king of Buganda, Uganda's central province. In order to prevent a royally inspired rebellion, different from the uprising in Kenya but equally threatening to the prestige of the empire, the governor arrested the king and flew him to exile in Britain. Throughout the decolonization of Africa Britain never appeared to learn that the arresting of moderate leaders was likely to make the victims both more radical and more popular. Thus a Ugandan king, who might have been seen by many as the indirect agent of colonial rule, as the representative of a limited ethnic section of Ugandan society, and as the voice of aristocratic privilege, came to be acclaimed as a nationalist politician. Once Britain had recognized its mistake it was too late to rectify it, and after his return the king led his own political party and eventually became president of an independent Uganda.

But the king-turned-politician was not the only leader seeking support for a decolonizing agenda in Uganda. A more democratic party of less privileged people grew up to rival the king's supporters and organized itself around the Roman Catholic missions that had traditionally opposed the Anglican royal court and the colonial establishment. The Catholic network enabled the democratic leaders to spread their message beyond the central kingdom and gain sufficient support to form a national government that ruled not only central Buganda but also the rival kingdoms of the south and the republican communities of the north. The north, however, had its own politicians, led by teachers and civil servants who formed a people's congress. This congress sought to build a unified Ugandan nation, rather than a federal one, but in order to win power it had to form an alliance with the king and allow his followers some constitutional concessions. In the final colonial election this coalition of diverse interests won a parliamentary majority in 1962 and the congress leader, Milton Obote, became prime minister. Three years later he broke the pact, drove the king once more into exile, and grasped further power.

The first round of decolonization in Uganda, in 1962, had been largely a constitutional decolonization in which the upper layer of British rule had been peeled away and the second layer of favoured aristocrats and bureaucrats took over the management of an otherwise little-changed system. One striking feature of continuity was the survival of the Asian merchant class, which continued to present the face of foreign influence in the village world of Uganda's peasants. Since shopkeepers and cotton buyers had been unacceptable representatives of colonial capitalism, and stimulants to a national awakening, it was surprising that they had not been seriously challenged for their alleged exploitation of "the people" or for the racial distinctiveness that made them such an easy target. But Asian traders provided services, transport, material goods and consumer credit, which enhanced the quality of rural life, albeit at a cost. The state could not offer such facilities and the black politicians and administrators came to be seen less as providers of services and more as collectors of taxes. They had won the decolonization elections on the single platform of self-government and once this had been achieved their cupboard was bare of further political offering. So government was identified as a source of jobs, salaries, security, contracts, gratuities and general profit for politicians and their cohorts of favoured clients. Good politicians, however, needed to keep an eye on all sections of society and keep challengers at bay with adequate rewards. If these rewards were illegitimate or corrupt it did not matter greatly; indeed, it might give senior politicians a firmer hold over those who accepted illegal fruits of office. The section of society that it was most important to satisfy in any relatively weak state, in Africa as elsewhere, was the army. This the Ugandan politicians, like so many of their contemporaries, failed to do. In 1971 Obote was overthrown by his own army, which was anxious to preserve its share of the spoils of state. The king's men were jubilant but their jubilation was short lived and the regime of General Idi Amin turned into a tyranny that brought African politics into gruesome disrepute.

The assumption of power by the Ugandan army in 1971 brought about a realignment of the forces that had struggled for control of the British heritage, as well as bringing a new force to the fore. The power of the north was reduced with the departure of Obote from the presidency. The politicians of the centre recovered some temporary advantage, although their king had died in exile. The new force came from the margins of the nation, or, indeed, from beyond the margins in the territories of Sudan where the British had occasionally recruited their soldiers. These soldiers owed debts to no one and set about the process of personal enrichment. Their shrewd if brutal general recognized that once state offices had been redistributed the next greatest source of wealth lay in the hands of Asian merchants. Merchants were unpopular, Asians were racially foreign, and the army rightly expected to win popular support by challenging them. In the name of nationalism it launched a second round of "decolonization" and gave the entire community of Asian settlers, immigrants, and expatriates notice to leave the country. Many of them fled to Britain where they painstakingly reconstructed their way of life by running small shops, newsagents and post offices. In Uganda their assets were taken over by soldiers, but the soldiers had none of the skills necessary to manage rural businesses, satisfy peasant wants, and keep national exports flowing. The politics of plunder soon turned inward and the soldiers indiscriminately exploited black Ugandans once the foreigners had gone. When the army was finally driven from office with some help from neighbouring Tanzania, it proved impossible to revive the fatally wounded postcolonial state and an intermittent civil war delayed reconstruction until 1986.

Royal and aristocratic politics may have played a role in Uganda that made the reconciliation of rival interest groups more difficult, and opened the way to power-broking by soldiers who cleverly won support from different factions until the nation's resources had been conspicuously squandered. In the two neighbouring kingdoms of Burundi and Rwanda, however, the politics of decolonization were even more destructive of human life than they became under army rule in Uganda. The two kingdoms, fertile and very densely populated, had been conquered by Germany during the scramble for Africa. When Germany was driven out of Africa during the First World War the kingdoms were placed in the custody of Belgium, which governed them with the help of an historic aristocracy calling themselves Tutsi. As the prospect of decolonization came closer the popular majority, calling themselves Hutu, expected to rise from their peasant poverty and gain democratic rights and equality of opportunity. That expectation, however, was hard to realize. Colonialism had left no institutions for resolving conflicts of interest peaceably. Granting independence did not bring greater social harmony, or create new wealth, or reconcile the aristocracy to losing the traditional status they had preserved under colonial rule. Independence therefore brought attempted revolutions and class warfare to picturesque mountain valleys at the very centre of Africa. For many decolonization and its aftermath meant sudden death. In both kingdoms revolution and counter-revolution swung back and forth as the

49

men of violence tried to commandeer power and property. The high-land fringe of eastern Africa proved as tragically difficult to turn into recognizable states as did the lowland fringe of the Somali coast.

The contrast between the dying mountain states of Burundi and Rwanda and the huge, half-empty republic of Tanzania, where so many sought havens of survival in refugee camps, could not be more complete. Yet Tanzania, like the mountain kingdoms, had originally been conquered by imperial Germany in the 1880s. When Germany was defeated in the African campaigns of the First World War Britain became the trustee in charge of the territory. Some continuity of German colonial practice was retained, in particular the use of Swahili as a lingua franca throughout a huge country with dozens of local languages. The spread of Swahili through colonial schools was designed to facilitate colonial administration, but it incidentally also facilitated political mobilization and the growth of national consciousness. In much of Africa the new politicians had to make their speeches, however patriotic or inflammatory, in the language of their oppressor, but in colonial Tanzania they could do so in Swahili and be widely understood. Politics in Tanzania reached the grass-roots more readily, and political discourse was less elitist, than in many countries. Democratic socialism of the kind practised in Britain after the Second World War appealed to Tanzanian politicians, and their leader, Julius Nyerere, won the nickname of Mwalimu, "the teacher", a term of reverence in Islamic culture and badge of achievement in colonial society. A scholar-politician, he translated Shakespeare's *Julius Caesar* into Swahili.

Nyerere the teacher became the father of his nation, but not without some obstruction. Education was a controversial feature of the colonial legacy. Students who went beyond the level of primary education in Swahili to secondary and university education in English gained enormously in status and influence. The British needed their skills but felt threatened by their political ambitions. Since Britain held Tanzania on trust for the United Nations, it had to take care not to crush African aspirations too strongly, but at the same time it wished to avoid encouraging nationalism in a manner that might incite neighbouring Kenyans to demand premature independence. Access to higher education was therefore limited, as it was in Kenya, and no colonial university was built in Tanzania. Selected students were permitted to go to university in Uganda, but they were not encouraged to study law – a subject that might enhance their political and constitutional skills in challenging the British right to rule in Africa. Ironically, access to education became a problem for the politicians too. They wanted to create a state that would serve the people without fear or favour and would treat all citizens equally. To achieve this they needed an educated bureaucracy to provide services that would otherwise be supplied by profiteers who served only those who rewarded them best. These ideals of equality and public service won the votes that gained Tanzania its independence. However, the new government employees expected to be well paid for their skills and aspired to the middle-class standards of comfort that their colonial predecessors had enjoyed. The teacher-president preached against inequality and exploitation and set an example of modest living that was unusual among postcolonial politicians. Tanzania's democratic ideals enabled the country to progress more smoothly than most and even to absorb peacefully its Asian immigrants and a few surviving white settlers. Decolonization, nevertheless, did suffer a few hiccoughs.

First, soon after independence the army went on strike for better pay and conditions and threatened to mutiny if it was not satisfied. Democratic parliamentarians did not know how to deal with restive soldiers and decided to swallow their nationalist pride; they invited Britain to return to quell the unruly behaviour of men who had so recently served unquestioningly under British officers. The second and much more serious hiccough came from the offshore island of Zanzibar. Although largely peopled by Africans from the mainland, Zanzibar was ruled by an immigrant dynasty from southern Arabia. The sultan had been "protected" by Britain during the colonial era, but when Britain withdrew he was overthrown by a revolution that challenged the privileges of the Arab elite. The revolutionary leaders threatened to hitch their fortunes to the Soviet Union, a prospect that so dismayed the United States that it invited Tanzania to annex the island. This was promptly done but created a running sore that absorbed far more of Tanzania's political energies than could be spared. In particular it detracted from the much more urgent task of rural development on the mainland, a task that proved the third hiccough of decolonization. The policy of Tanzanian rural development was called *ujamaa* and was designed to bring health, education and productivity to the peasant majority. The political will, however, was matched neither by the technical skills nor by the financial resources required for success. For a time the government pursued the policy without the democratic consent of the people they aimed to assist, and foreign sympathy for Tanzania's ideals of village development was diminished. Nevertheless, Tanzania remained one of the most stable of former colonies in Africa. It had the least polarized discrepancies of wealth and avoided military interference in its policymaking. Most strikingly of all, it continued to test, and replace, its politicians by due electoral process.

While the offshore island of Zanzibar was being absorbed by its onshore neighbour, the deep-sea islands of the Indian Ocean began seeking their own paths to independence. The Seychelles islands – with a mixed French, African and British ancestry – gained independence, changed government, and invited Tanzania to send a police force to maintain sufficient order to keep out exiled politicians and bring in dollar-paying tourists. The Comoros islands, with a Muslim tradition and an economy linked to the French perfume industry, won independence, quarrelled among themselves, were invaded by armed mercenaries, and split into colonized and decolonized factions. Mauritius, named after a Dutch prince who had once dominated the ocean trade, was colonized primarily by French-speaking Indians but had been ruled since the Napoleonic wars by Britain. Its sugar industry gave it the viability to become an independent member of both the commonwealth and the Organization of African Unity. Neighbouring Réunion, by contrast, did not seek independence but a closer relationship with France, eventually becoming an overseas French territory with significant financial subsidies. The last and much the largest of the islands off eastern Africa to seek a new future was Madagascar.

The decolonization of Madagascar was intimately linked to the campaigns of the Second World War. In 1940 the French colonial administration on the island, in common with the French west African administration in Dakar, but in contrast to the French equatorial African administration in Brazzaville, chose to support Marshal Pétain rather than General de Gaulle. As a result, Britain invaded Madagascar, as it had invaded Ethiopia, in order to remove a hostile colonial regime. The British brought with them a representative of de Gaulle but effectively remained in control of the island until 1946. When the British finally withdrew, many people in Madagascar aspired to be given self-government. They were dismayed that the departure of the British brought instead a restoration of French colonial rule. A nominal entitlement to elect two members of the French parliament to represent Madagascar's interests was no substitute for freedom. Soon after the French return a rebellion broke out on the island, which far exceeded the Kenyan rebellion of 1952 in its scale and intensity. Adopting the military determination later witnessed in Algeria, France crushed the rebellion with the loss of 100,000 lives. The political repression was so fierce that two former members of parliament were condemned to death by colonial law courts.

The restoration of formal French political authority in Madagascar lasted barely ten years. Several factors combined to reopen the independence debate. The Catholic Church, fearful of the spread of communism, softened its old mission support for unreformed colonial rule. The emergence of Egypt as the African voice from the Third World, and the decolonization of Morocco and Tunisia, gave nationalists new hope. When a constitutional framework for the tropical colonies was approved in Paris in 1956, new political parties sprang up on the island. In the towns nationalists were more radical than those in the countryside and were suspicious of the controlled decolonization that de Gaulle came to offer. Compromises were made and in 1960 Madagascar, like other French tropical colonies, accepted the terms available. Moderate policies enabled settlers to remain on the island, gave French commerce and industry a privileged place in the economy, and made French education the cultural heritage of the ruling elite. Independence brought peace if not prosperity.

CHAPTER FOUR

Private enterprise and peasant rebellions in west-central Africa

West-central Africa, stretching from the deserts and savannas of Lake Chad, through the great equatorial forests of Congo and Zaire, to the deserts and savannas of the upper Zambezi, bore some resemblance to the neighbouring regions of northern, western and eastern Africa. It contained old kingdoms such as Adamawa in the French zone, Lunda in the Belgian zone, and Kongo in the Portuguese zone, which all played a role in the politics of decolonization. It had Creole communities such as Duala in the French zone, Boma in the Belgian zone and Benguela in the Portuguese zone which tried with greater or less success to protect their old social and commercial status during and after the colonial era. In all three zones virulent peasant rebellions resembling those of Kenya or Madagascar broke out during the transition from colonial rule to independence. But the equatorial regions of west-central Africa also had a distinctive colonial heritage of their own. Each of the three imperial powers had delegated an unusual degree of authority over large and sparsely peopled tracts of country to private colonizing companies, which were given charters that entitled them to extract wealth and exploit people with minimal supervision. This entrepreneurial form of colonization brought a tradition of widespread human violence to west-central Africa, which probably exceeded that experienced in any of the other four regions of Africa. The legacy of this violence was profoundly felt in the years of the colonial aftermath.

The first zone to seek independence was the French one, consisting of four equatorial colonies and the former German territory of

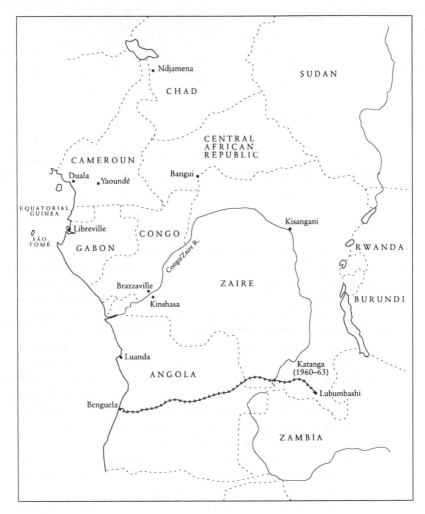

West-Central Africa

Cameroun. The symptoms of local autonomy emerged in 1940 when French merchants and administrators had to decide how to survive the Second World War when cut off from occupied France by allied navies in the Atlantic and by shortages of vehicles and petrol in the Sahara. Reluctantly and pragmatically, they decided that, despite their hostility to the British, Nigeria provided their best chance of retaining economic contact with the outside world. They also decided, despite their racial prejudices, that the West Indian governor of Chad, Félix Eboué, was their most talented administrator. With this black leadership the equatorial territories opted to support "Free France" and in 1944 de Gaulle visited their federal capital at Brazzaville and offered his loyal African subjects post-war citizenship and integration with France. For ten years France invested development funds in equatorial Africa in the expectation that the colonies would be profitable and would assist the economic recovery of France. By the mid 1950s, however, wealth creation in Europe had outstripped the prospects in tropical Africa; the defence of colonies elsewhere was proving costly and embarrassing; the British were encouraging Africans to think of self-government rather than metropolitan integration; and the United Nations was asking about the future of its wards in Cameroun, most of whom had been entrusted to France but some of which were administered by Britain. French policy changed in equatorial Africa, as it did in western Africa, to one of controlled political decolonization with strong economic links to individual and independent republics.

The first and most difficult case for France to tackle was Cameroun. The country was almost as diverse in its cultural and ethnic make-up as neighbouring Nigeria. Moreover, the western part of Cameroun was under British colonial trusteeship and had been governed as part of Nigeria. Reintegrating those parts of the western provinces that wished to leave Nigeria, and rejoin a greater Cameroun that roughly covered the old German territory, presented one of the most delicate prospects of decolonization. In almost all other parts of Africa, including the partitioned German colony of Togo in western Africa, the latest colonial boundaries were preserved during the decolonizing process. In Cameroun two territories with contrasted French and British colonial traditions were brought together and the institutions of education, of justice, and of law enforcement had to be harmonized. The task was a sensitive one, highlighting the extent to which colonization had created cultural expectations in colonized societies. But integrating western Cameroun was not the only political reconciliation that Cameroun faced. Before independence the Bamileke people developed a political agenda of their own as entrepreneurial activists who had spread out from their crowded farms to become businessmen. Their success was such that they even challenged some of the immigrant business communities from Greece, Lebanon, Senegal and France. They moved to the towns, formed voluntary associations, developed self-help credit, and invested in taxis and small lorries. France decided that the Bamileke were becoming too radical in their economic ambitions and too powerful in their political appeal. When the Bamileke rebelled at the obstructions placed in their path, the French used military force to crush them with the loss of several thousand lives. In their place the French sponsored a much more conservative political movement that was rooted among the Muslim aristocracy of the north and notably in the emirate of Adamawa, which was historically linked to the northern emirates of Nigeria. The party leader, Ahidjo, was sufficiently astute to balance the internal political interests of his country and avoid offending his entourage of French advisers. After independence Cameroun became one of the most successful of France's African clients and expanded the plantation economy it had inherited from the German period. In due course mineral wealth was discovered, which enabled members of the new political elite to reward themselves without initially causing unquenched protests from farmers or wage-earners.

A similar process of trial and error led the other French colonies towards independence, although with less political continuity and stability than that achieved in Cameroun. Decolonization brought an increase in French investment and French expatriate personnel to the Central African region after 1960 as the new governments expanded the role of the state from colonial minimalism to a much wider responsibility for education, economic planning and transport infrastructure for private industries. In the north potential investors were attracted by mineral prospects in Chad, but neither the politicians nor the French were able to hold the country together after independence and war-lords ruled shifting fiefs with funds and weapons supplied by foreign supporters. In the diamond-rich Central African Republic, French politicians and businessmen manipulated local interest groups openly and even learnt to live with, and profit from, one of the most unsavoury of Africa's soldier-politicians. Jean Bedel Bokassa had few credentials as a liberator, having fought for the French in Algeria, but when he returned home he succeeded in gaining power, using the national treasury to crown himself "emperor" after the style of Napoleon. Eventually his cruel excesses caused the French discreetly to remove him to comfortable exile and restore one of their former political clients, David Dacko, to presidential office in 1979. Further south the survival of French interests in Congo involved even more astute footwork as politicians across the spectrum from the Catholic Church to the Marxist officers' clubs played musical chairs with ministerial office. They financed the state by the sale of tropical timber and iron ore to French companies of the type that had played such a key role in creating the colony in the first place.

The smallest and richest of France's equatorial colonies, and the one where the least power was transferred to African politicians in the process of decolonization, was Gabon. An old-style logging colony that sold tropical hardwoods, Gabon had been founded as a settlement for liberated slaves and had later attracted one of Europe's most famous medical missionaries, Albert Schweitzer. After independence it became important to France because it could alleviate France's acute shortage of industrial energy in two ways, by supplying uranium as nuclear fuel for the electrical industry and by supplying crude oil to be refined for the transport industry. Such was the wealth of Gabon that when France's appointee as local president was threatened with dismissal by rival local interests, de Gaulle's army invaded the new republic to restore the chosen postcolonial order. The next president of Gabon took the Africanized name of Omar Bongo and adopted Islam to mask his French culture, but France maintained control, and economic and diplomatic policy continued to be filtered through the French embassy, which was closely linked to the presidential palace. The wealth of mineral exports after independence drained half the population to the capital, Libreville, and the country had to import food from France and labour from the neighbouring Spanish colony of Equatorial Guinea. When Spain later granted independence to Equatorial Guinea, the territory became closely associated with Gabon and adopted the French equatorial currency, a currency that enhanced French financial control over the whole equatorial region. Gabon also became a trading partner of, and a haven of refuge for, the politicians of São Tomé, the offshore island decolonized by Portugal in 1975. Neocolonialism in Gabon had acquired a tone of imperial expansionism. Libreville even became a supply centre for the giant American oil platforms off the coast of Angola, far to the south. But decolonization had brought extraction and consumption rather than freedom of choice and development of potential.

The relationship between politicians and prospectors that seemed to dominate the decolonizing agenda of French equatorial Africa was also important in Zaire, the million-square-mile colony that was called the Congo State before 1908, the Belgian Congo to 1960 and the Democratic Republic of Congo-Kinshasa until 1971. But whereas the decolonization of French equatorial Africa was controlled almost exclusively by France, the decolonization of Belgian equatorial Africa became a responsibility shared by the entire world community. Both the superpowers, Russia and America, became deeply involved in trying to control the process. Radical African states led by Egypt tried to support one political tendency while conservative African states discreetly encouraged by South Africa supported another. Ghana offered assistance in the hope that Zaire would become one of its pan-African partners. Belgium tried to protect its citizens and its investments by direct and indirect interventions while Britain, France and Portugal speculated anxiously about how to safeguard their own adjacent spheres of influence. Lastly, the United Nations, using troops from ex-colonies as far away as Ireland and India, embarked on its biggest ever attempt to bring order to a disintegrated nation. At the end of the day, however, it was investment managers who regained control of Zaire. The Belgian colony had been a giant interlocking complex of mining and plantation companies held together by an armed police force. The republic of Zaire that emerged from the eventful decolonizing process was very similar. Although the plantations dwindled, the mines survived under the control of foreign financial and engineering interests and paid the state royalties that funded the wellbeing of a ruling army managed by the entrepreneurial general Mobutu Sese Seko, who became the country's most successful businessman.

The constitutional politics of decolonization in late colonial Zaire involved four distinct political traditions, associated with four widely separated regions and led by four sharply contrasted personalities with strong political views. In the west the political tradition was cultural. Its twin roots were royal ethnicity and black Christianity. The ethnicity was associated with the late medieval kingdom of Kongo and a cultural association of Kongo-speakers was led by Joseph Kasavubu. The Christian dimension was associated with the messianic preacher Simon Kimbangu, who spent 30 years in a colonial prison for inciting Kongo-speakers to believe in the equality of black people. As decolonization approached, the preacher's son set up an independent church that challenged not only the racism of the state, but also the collaborationist stance of white-run mission churches, both Catholic and Protestant. Although the cultural tradition was elitist, it sparked the imagination of popular aspiration and in 1959 riots broke out in the western city of Kinshasa (then called Léopoldville), when the Belgians seemed to be reluctant to accept that a tide of decolonization was sweeping down from the north. The riots triggered a volte-face in Belgian politics. Colonial officials and metropolitan politicians had all assumed that decolonization required a long preparation and that they had 30 years in which to groom their black successors. The riots caused them to realize that no such preparation or grooming was possible unless they were prepared to use expensive military force to stem the tide of African liberation. Such expenditure would have been so unpopular in Belgium that the government decided to decolonize in one year and to seek instant candidates for the political succession.

The second political tradition in colonial Zaire was bureaucratic, and it found its leader in the north. Although the black bureaucracy in Belgian Africa was large, it was junior in status and decision-making remained in the hands of white officials. The educational system had trained large numbers of literate typists to work in private enterprise and government service but had not given subject peoples access to managerial training. Even when the Catholic Church set up a colonial university, the large majority of its students were the children of white officials. Political aspirations in Zaire were therefore mobilized by post-office counter-clerks rather than by civil service lawyers. The northern leader of the post-office workers was Lumumba, and his followers were young men in a hurry who wanted rapid promotion to situations of prestige from which they were being excluded by white expatriates. The bureaucratic tradition of colonial politics became more radical than the cultural one and the Belgians soon found that they could not ignore it. When they tested political opinion by the introduction of electoral politics with universal suffrage, the followers of Lumumba gained a significant regional and ideological foothold in the newly established parliament. In 1960 power was shared between the the moderate cultural tradition of the west and the radical bureaucratic tradition of the north. Kasavubu became president and Lumumba prime minister.

Thirdly, there was the political business tradition in Zaire. Its leader was a politician from the east, Moïse Tshombe, who came from the royal house of Lunda and had built up his own black business in the marginal economic niches that white entrepreneurs had neglected. He was ideologically opposed to the radicalism of the northern politicians and culturally alienated by the haughty distinctiveness of those of the west. Worse still, the eastern politicians found that there was no real position of influence for them in the power-sharing deal that had been agreed in the new parliament. Within a fortnight of Belgian decolonization they therefore decided to secede and create their own independent republic of Katanga. In so doing they attracted very powerful support. The richest mining houses, based in Katanga and producing a strategically significant proportion of the world's copper, supported Tshombe and negotiated railway rights out of the rebel province via white-ruled neighbouring colonies. The local Belgian population supported the secession and gained discreet but powerful support from some political interests in Belgium. But Tshombe's breakaway also attracted very powerful opposition. Many of the mine workers in Katanga were immigrants from the Luba kingdoms of south Zaire and they felt very threatened by the political preferences given to Tshombe's ethnic allies. Secession triggered off an ethnic war that led to mass flight and greatly increased the levels of anxiety about the future in the rest of Zaire. Equally dramatically, the United States decided to oppose the business-backed secessionist regime, fearing that the break-up of Zaire might create unwelcome opportunities for Soviet intervention. The crisis was referred to the United Nations, which decided that the rebellion should be ended and that the wealthy mining province should be reintegrated into Zaire. Implementing this policy required three years of armed intervention by a large international force. During the struggle Lumumba was kidnapped and murdered and his radical bureaucratic tradition was partially superseded by a violent populist tradition.

The emergence of a fourth political tradition in the decolonizing politics of Zaire was particularly notable in the rural south where its most prominent leader was Pierre Mulele. Under the Belgians peasant producers had not prospered greatly, but they knew what to expect and were provided with transport services and market outlets. Decolonization led them to anticipate new wealth, but instead they found that the limited security they had previously experienced crumbled away. Rural standards of living dropped and peasants saw that independence was bringing benefits only to the wage earners of the towns. As rural poverty spread anger was mobilized and populist politicians railed against the townsmen who had highjacked the national heritage. The murderous peasant rebellion led by Mulele was confined to the south, but similar rebellions imitated it in the east and the north. Angry bands of youths even captured the city of Kisangani, Lumumba's former base, and killed members of the bureaucratic class whom they blamed for their disappointments. The prospective disintegration of the whole country brought about a dramatic realignment of politics. In 1964 Tshombe, the secessionist eastern politician who had been driven out by the United Nations, was brought back to Zaire, this time to become prime minister of the whole country with his office in Kinshasa, the capital against which he had fought so long and hard. Tshombe recruited a mercenary army among his former white supporters and drove the peasant rebels out of the towns, thus enabling colonial enterprises to reopen for business in moderate postcolonial safety. A year later the western city politicians, led by President Kasavubu, felt safe enough to depose Tshombe again. Within weeks, however, they themselves had been deposed by Mobutu, a politician from the army rather than from any of the four ideological traditions that had hitherto disputed the Belgian inheritance.

The emergence of the army as the heir to the Belgians in the decolonization of Zaire ought not to have caused much surprise. The role of the military had been central both to colonial government and to the decolonizing process. Mobutu's rise to power had several strands of logic. Already in 1960 the Zaire army had shown its ambitions, although these were essentially seen as ambitions of opportunity common to all decolonized sections of society wanting to rid themselves of well-paid white superiors and take over their status and income for themselves. Mutineers during the first days of independence were talked back to their barracks by peace-brokers, although Belgian paratroops was kept at the ready. During the United Nations operation Zaire soldiers saw black officers from other African countries taking political responsibility for peacekeeping and naturally aspired to gain such influence for themselves once the international force had withdrawn. Mobutu, a former soldier working then as a journalist, had played a small political role in 1960 when Lumumba appointed him chief of staff of the army and Mobutu in turn colluded with the dismissal of Lumumba, if not with his subsequent murder. Mobutu's success, however, was not just as a military leader but also as business negotiator. International firms were increasingly willing to bribe new politicians in Africa as part of the process of buying influence in decolonized states. They had greater success in Zaire than in most ex-colonies. Once in power Mobutu licensed the great mining companies to dig copper and diamonds as before. He also manipulated small Greek, Indian and Portuguese businesses in his own interests or replaced them with a new African business class closely associated with the army. Mobutu's political acumen also made him a skilled operator on the world stage, winning him 30 years of supreme power and periodic support from America, France, South Africa and even China.

In 1960 Belgium had decided not to send a military expedition to Africa to preserve its colonial assets and to protect the hundred thousand citizens who were working there on its behalf. In the neighbouring colony of Angola, Portugal made the opposite choice. In 1961 it did decide to send an expeditionary army conscripted in Europe to Africa. The object was to retain Portugal's largest colonial possession and to protect the lives of a hundred thousand settlers and expatriates from an anti-colonial rebellion. There were several reasons for the conflicting responses of Belgium and Portugal to the sudden advent of the decolonizing revolution in west-central Africa. The first was that Belgium was a democracy and had to take careful note of political opinion with regard to policy. It also had to respond to national sensitivity with regard to the deployment of young conscripts whose lives were put at risk. Portugal, by contrast, was a dictatorship, and although public opinion had to be nurtured and conscription was unpopular, any open protest could be censored out of the press and any politician bold enough to speak out could be cast into prison.

The second difference was that Belgium was an industrial nation at the heart of a rapidly developing European community and could offer to maintain commercial, industrial and financial ties with Zaire on competitive terms. Portugal, by contrast, was primarily an agrarian country on the most remote and poorest fringe of Western Europe and feared that Germany, and other non-colonizing industrial nations, were waiting to seize opportunities in any colonies that Portugal might relinquish. Thirdly, the United States, having encouraged the colonial powers to withdraw from northern and western

Africa in the 1950s, recognized by 1961 that such a withdrawal was liable to draw in Soviet influence, as in the case of Zaire. Moreover, the United States needed strategic facilities on the Portuguese islands in the Atlantic and so was persuaded to reverse its stance of "Africa for the Africans" and encourage Portugal to crush the rebellion and restore colonial authority in Angola. Angola's politicians had to wait more than ten years for their decolonizing opportunity.

The politicians who sought independence in Angola, like those of Zaire, belonged to several distinct traditions. These traditions were woven by threads of ideology, belief and language into three separate political parties. None of these parties had a sufficient commitment to a national, as opposed to a sectional, political agenda to inherit sole recognition as the convincing voice of the anti-colonial struggle. The first of the parties, the Movement for the Popular Liberation of Angola (MPLA), was rooted in the tradition of government service and the waged bureaucracy of the colonial capital at Luanda. It focused on the state as servant of the people, an ideology that made it appear radical in its policies of national ownership and state capitalism but also safeguarded tenured salaries for its members. The leaders of the popular movement came from competing strands of colonial history. The old black Creoles dated back to the seventeenth century, spoke Portuguese as their mother tongue, belonged to the Catholic Church, and had an old military tradition of service to the state that was revived during the liberation struggle and gave them great influence in the party. A second strand of the popular movement came from the city hinterland where Mbundu-speaking peoples had gained educational opportunities through a network of Methodist missions. Many moved to the city to find ways out of their peasant environment while retaining links with their kith and kin, which formed an important feature of the party's strength and legitimacy. The third distinctive strand was made up of the sons of white settlers and colonial officials who had failed to find white brides in the colonies and so had married Africans. These people of mixed ancestry, although given educational opportunities by their white fathers, felt increasingly marginalized by a post-war influx of immigrants from Europe. In the late 1950s some of them joined the popular movement and even became its leading policy-makers, planning the multiracial socialist society that they expected to emerge from the war of liberation.

The second ideological tradition was found in the Front for the National Liberation of Angola (FNLA) and was very different from that of the popular movement. Its leaders had no experience of public service and the elite worked instead in the private sector. More than that, the members of the liberation front belonged to sections of Angolan society that had always seen their business opportunities as lying in Kinshasa, in colonial Zaire, rather than in Luanda, Angola's capital, where jobs as tailors, taxi drivers, cobblers, street vendors, barmaids and butchers' boys were monopolized by poor and often illiterate whites who had migrated to Africa from the backlands of Portugal. The members of the FNLA did not speak Mbundu or Portuguese, like the people of Luanda, but used the many Kongo dialects that straddled the colonial border and learnt French to gain access to business opportunities in Kinshasa. On both sides of the frontier they belonged to the Baptist Church and a Protestant work ethic enhanced their commitment to capitalism. When the colonial war ended in Angola in 1974 the businessmen from the north lost no time in moving to Luanda, where they not only replaced the departing petty white traders and artisans but used their capital, and that of their sponsors, to buy up housing, land, industry, printing presses and radio stations. They also made a political bid for power in the capitals but that failed and they contented themselves with running the private, parallel, sector of economy while the core fell into the socialist hands of their rivals in the popular movement.

The political traditions of the national union (Union for the National Independence of the Totality of Angola, UNITA) were different again from those of the liberation front and the popular movement. The national union's main support came from the old merchant kingdoms of the central highlands of Angola. Some of its leaders had aristocratic connections and nearly all of them spoke the highland languages of the Ovimbundu. A modernizing factor creating political cohesion across ethnic factions was that many of UNITA's leaders had attended Presbyterian schools, or been treated in Presbyterian hospitals, run by missionaries from Switzerland and Canada. Some had also developed a long-distance network of camaraderie and communication by working on the Benguela railway that brought Zaire copper across the whole breadth of Angola to the Atlantic ports. In its search for an ideology of liberation that would be attractive to the peasant population of the highlands, Angola's third force turned not to America, which supported the liberation front, nor to Russia, which supported the popular movement, but to China. Angola's peasants, however, were individualists, their leaders were capitalists, and China had little to offer in the way of material assistance. The national union therefore made secret overtures to the Portuguese, offering to help them to eradicate left-wing guerrillas from the war zones in return for favoured treatment in a compromise settlement of the colonial struggle. The deal sowed the seeds for many more years of conflict in the highlands.

The liberation war in Angola had two intense phases, separated by a long period of virtual stalemate in which the colony remained on a war footing but few casualties occurred. The first phase was in 1961. The popular movement, stirred by peasant starvation and rebellion in the Mbundu cotton fields and inspired by the sudden decolonization of Belgian Africa, tried to liberate its imprisoned leaders in an attack on Luanda gaol. The consequence was an outburst of violence in which white vigilante gangs sought out and killed educated Africans whom they feared might deprive them of their jobs or, worse still, might aspire to a political independence that would send them back to peasant poverty in Europe. A month later a second uprising occurred, this time in the northern sphere of influence of the liberation front, when unpaid coffee pickers demanded their arrears of wages and were fired upon by planters. This time the panic was even more widespread and violent; hundreds of whites and thousands of blacks were killed in the coffee plantations, and tens of thousands of frightened refugees escaped to Zaire where they stayed for more than ten years. Portugal recovered control with a large metropolitan army partly equipped with American weapons of counter-insurgency. A new economic policy brought an expansion of the plantation economy, an influx of new immigrants, the development of rich offshore oil wells, and the growth of local consumer industries. Moderate economic wellbeing, even among Africans, postponed the second phase of active fighting until 1975, but by then the conflict was not about liberation itself but about who should inherit the spoils in a colony that had become rich and successful.

The decolonization of Angola was quite different from any other decolonization in Africa. By 1974 the politicians had failed in their bid for freedom and there was fratricidal conflict not merely between the three parties but also within them, to the great chagrin of their

67

foreign supporters, who had begun to despair of Angola. Decolonization came about almost accidentally in Angola; the Portuguese army refused to continue to fight in Portugal's two other colonial wars, in Guinea and Mozambique, and so toppled the ruling dictatorship in Lisbon. At first it was thought that little change would occur in Angola, that the settler population that had risen to a quarter of a million would remain to manage the economic miracle, and that a coalition government of three parties would be established in which white influence retained the lever of power. The parties, however, could not agree either on policy or on power-sharing as they converged on the capital from their highlands, their guerrilla camps and their exile. The exiles from the north called on Zaire to help them with regiments from Mobutu's army. The men from the highlands called on South Africa to help them by sending in commandos from the south. The guerrillas from the camps called on Cuba to make good its claim to be the champion of Third World freedom and fly airborne troops in from the Caribbean. The settlers decided to leave, taking with them everything that they could pack in air crates and destroying much that they had to leave behind. The new Portuguese military government in Lisbon could not decide what to do, and so on 11 November 1975 it withdrew the last colonial governor who was shipped out on a gunboat under cover of darkness bequeathing independence "to the people of Angola as a whole".

For 20 years the politicians tried to find a postcolonial settlement that would satisfy the people of Angola as a whole. They failed, and Angola became a focus for active Cold War confrontation between the superpowers. The Soviet Union sold military equipment to the popular movement to shore up its power in its urban and coastal enclaves even when it had little support in the neglected countryside. South Africa supplied weapons to the national union, thereby enhancing its own anti-communist credentials with the West at a time when it was otherwise strongly criticized for its oppressive racial policies at home. American business siphoned off the oil and paid royalties to the popular movement government while American politicians built air bases in Zaire and allowed them to be used in support of the opposition national union. By 1990, however, the Cold War was over, the Soviet Union had withdrawn, America had almost lost interest in Africa, South Africa had recognized the need for political reform, and the Angolans were left to solve their own dispute with reduced interference. Two civil wars occurred. In 1991 the national union captured many of the rural areas and the popular movement captured most of the towns. They signed a peace and ran an election, which the popular movement won in reasonably free and fair fashion. The national union thereupon rearmed and this time conquered the provincial cities, causing widespread destruction and preventing the distribution of food to starving areas. The popular movement rearmed in its turn, bringing even heavier and more sophisticated weapons to Africa, and with even greater bloodshed and destruction recaptured the provincial towns that it had lost. A ceasefire was laboriously negotiated by the United Nations in 1994, but much of decolonized Angola lay in ruins.

CHAPTER FIVE

White power and black response in southern Africa

Southern Africa is the core of Anglo-Saxon Africa and the region that attracted the lion's share of British investments in Africa. It is in southern Africa that two million white, English-speaking descendants of settlers created colonial communities, and colonial-style states, during the nineteenth and twentieth centuries. But southern Africa had two older colonial traditions that survived alongside the Anglo-Saxon one. In the east, Portuguese colonists from Europe and Asia began to settle in the sixteenth century and in the nineteenth century conquered the large coastal colony of Mozambique. Although the colony became closely integrated into the economy of surrounding British Africa, using British coinage and driving on the left-hand side of the road, Mozambique nevertheless had a colonial culture and language of its own and when decolonized remained a distinctively Latin part of southern Africa.

In the west of southern Africa the British were also preceded by the Dutch, whose descendants formed two of the largest colonial sections of the population of southern Africa, one white Afrikaners and the other "coloured" Afrikaans-speakers. Britain took over the colonial management of the Dutch colony at the Cape during the Napoleonic wars and in 1820 began planting English settlers there. Half a century later they granted self-government to the British and Dutch settlers in the Cape colony, together with a few coloured and black voters who had gained approved property and educational qualifications. Decolonization therefore began in southern Africa before the colonial conquest had been completed in tropical Africa. By 1899 all of south-

Southern Africa

ern Africa, with the exception of German Namibia and the partial exception of Portuguese Mozambique, had been brought under British control. Self-government had been recognized by Britain not only in the Cape, but also in a second British colony in Natal and in two Afrikaner republics, the Orange Free State and the Transvaal. The Transvaal, however, claimed not only the right to self-government but also the sovereign right to conduct its own international affairs with regard to the development of the gold-mining industry. This Britain would not permit and in 1899 war broke out between Afrikaners and Britons. By 1902 Britain had invaded southern Africa with the largest and most costly army that it ever deployed in Africa, and had conquered the so-called "Boer" republics and their gold mines.

After the Anglo–Boer war self-government was rapidly restored to the white settlers and in 1910 a union of the two former republics and the two former colonies was created and given "dominion status" in the British empire. Black Africans, however, were excluded from politics in all but the Cape province and even there black voting rights were restricted and were eliminated altogether within half a century, leaving the union with a political system exclusively controlled by a white electorate. The union was recognized by the world community as a legitimate sovereign state and after 1931 the British Parliament surrendered its last right of intervention and its last opportunity to protect the rights of black subject peoples. By 1961 the rights of South Africa's black subjects were again in the news. Decolonization in southern Asia and western Africa had created a multiracial commonwealth that was unable to accept as a member an Afrikaner-ruled republic that retained colonial-style white political supremacy. A 30-year struggle eventually brought political reform, democratic power-sharing, and the readmission of South Africa to the commonwealth. Before that final twist of African decolonization, however, the politics of liberation were played out in eight other territories in southern Africa. Three were the small British protectorates, Lesotho, Swaziland and Botswana, whose kings and chiefs had been kept out ot the union by Britain and which were now partly restored to their pre-colonial status, although their subjects remained largely dependent on South African mining, manufacturing and farming for employment. One of the territories was the former German colony of Namibia, which had virtually become the fifth province of South Africa and was decolonized in 1990 as part of the process of change in South Africa itself. And three, together with the associated Portuguese colony of Mozambique, were the British territories of the Zambezi basin which had been hitched to the British empire by Cecil Rhodes and his British South Africa Company. It was these territories that presented Britain with its last, most difficult, and most protracted challenge of decolonization.

In 1953 Britain thought that controlled decolonization might best be achieved in the Zambezi basin by creating a federal structure similar to the old French federation in west Africa or to the British-sponsored union in South Africa. The three territories concerned were very different but from the imperial point of view complemented each other economically. The smallest and most populated was Malawi (Nyasaland), and it was expected to earn its place in the federation by exporting migrant labour to the other two territories from its crowded peasant villages. The largest and richest was Zambia (Northern Rhodesia), which had a small population and few educational opportunities for its people but owned the largest copper mines in British Africa. The most heavily colonized territory was Zimbabwe (Southern Rhodesia, later Rhodesia), which had a quarter of a million white settlers who planted tobacco and maize. They also controlled the coal mine that fuelled the long-distance railways throughout the region. The settlers had been given a semi-autonomous self-governing status after the First World War when they declined to join the union in South Africa but claimed for themselves constitutional privileges similar to those enjoyed by whites in the south. Forty years later they were willing to make small concessions to African political demands in exchange for improved access to the mineral wealth of Zambia and the labour resources of Malawi. The racial laws governing social intercourse in Zimbabwe were, however, only slightly modified to allow black bus drivers to drive white passengers, black customers to enter white post offices, and black undergraduates to lodge in university hostels within the segregated colonial city of Salisbury. The capital of the new Central Africa was to be located in this city and so the construction, trading and employment opportunities associated with big government came to the white-run businesses of the southern territory of the federation.

The British Central African Federation represented such an unequal partnership that it soon collapsed. In Malawi nationalists educated in the mission schools recalled the heroic anti-colonial resistance of their forefathers and demanded the end of a federation that brought them neither political self-esteem nor economic comfort. In 1959 they rebelled and white forces from Southern Rhodesia invaded and arrested the political leaders. British political opinion, however, saw this as an unwise if not unconstitutional move to support white power in southern Africa and to evade responsibility for the rights of black colonial subjects who were quite aware of the independence movement in western Africa. The transfer of power to Malawi politicians was accordingly negotiated over the next four years. A similar demand for freedom from white federal control immediately grew up in Zambia, but Britain was more reluctant to surrender residual power there lest it lose its alleged right to mineral royalties in the copper mines. Worse still, Britain feared that control of a strategic resource, important to the defence industry as well as to the economy, might fall under the influence of rival powers. Across the Zambian border in Zaire civil war and foreign intervention had not yet resolved the future of the northern half of the Central African belt of copper mines. International mining, however, took the longer view and advised that although African copper was commendably cheap because of the extremely low wages and insignificant social security paid to migrant workers, it was not irreplaceable. In 1964 Britain took the risk of transferring power to black Zambian politicians in the reasonable certainty that they would not have the strength to alter significantly the terms of trade in the copper industry to Britain's disadvantage. Although royalties were now paid to an African government and could be used to expand the educational system and finance the growth of the state, the basic economic reality of Zambia was unchanged. Farmers received little benefit from independence and the copper industry remained an economic enclave effectively run from South Africa with South African skilled labour and South African machinery.

When the northern territories of the British federation won black majority rule and at least a limited increase in their freedom of economic choice, the southern territory saw its sphere of influence shrinking and the wellbeing of its dominant settler community threatened. A liberal white prime minister from the mission tradition, who had put his faith in interracial partnership, had been replaced by increasingly intransigent white politicians who encouraged a siege mentality, spoke of the lifelong preservation of white supremacy, and offered very restricted constitutional opportunities to the black Zimbabwean leadership. The black politicians appealed to Britain to support them, offering stability and continuity under middle-class leadership provided that all communities, and not merely favoured elites and moderate minorities, be given access to the electoral franchise. White politicians responded by banning successive political parties and arresting black activists. The whites appealed to Britain in turn, offering to maintain what they termed "civilized" standards of government. Britain was unable to wring constitutional concessions from the Rhodesia Front of white supremacists and in 1965 its leader, Ian Smith, led a white rebellion against the British crown and unilaterally declared Rhodesia to be independent. Britain retaliated by cutting off financial services and blockading the Rhodesian harbours and oil terminals in Mozambique, but it was unwilling and unable to use military force against white rebels in the manner it might have done against black rebels in Africa. Six years of stalemate followed with black leaders held in prison or living in exile and British negotiators unable to find a compromise solution despite cloak-and-dagger meetings with the rebels on warships at sea. The quiescence of blacks and the obduracy of whites was partly brought about by a period of colonial prosperity not dissimilar to the prosperity that brought a lull in the Angolan liberation struggle in the same years. When cut off from their foreign suppliers Rhodesians developed their own self-reliant manufacturing industries, thus reducing the white need for imported consumer goods, and inducing a modest prosperity that quietened some black political aspirations.

The year 1970 began a decade of change that transformed racist Rhodesia into multiracial Zimbabwe in one of the hardest-fought struggles for decolonization seen outside Algeria. It began when the white regime persuaded itself, and also a new Conservative Government in London, that Zimbabweans would now be ready to accept a compromise constitution that gave them slow access to political preferment, guided by "loyal" black chiefs, rather than instant independence led by radical city politicians. The years of quiescence came to an abrupt end. While the established black politicians were still in gaol a nationwide protest movement was orchestrated by the black Methodist churchman Abel Muzorewa. The British Government reluctantly had to acknowledge that Africans would not accept independence without majority rule and the white rebellion carried on. Black protest now focused on Zimbabwean exiles and two political movements began to arm their followers in order to launch a war of liberation across the borders. Zapu, led by the old veteran Joshua Nkomo, had a base in Zambia where it trained a fairly conventional army with Soviet assistance and enjoyed the tacit British expectation that it would inherit Rhodesia and decolonize with a minimum of disruption to social structure, economic order and government services. The rival political movement, Zanu, was meanwhile taken over by the more radical Robert Mugabe and built a new base in Mozambique where it trained an irregular guerrilla army with Chinese ideas and weapons. Its policy was not to inherit the colonial system intact but to undermine it from its rural roots until it collapsed and could be replaced by an entirely new, more egalitarian, social and economic order. The ideal appealed to the young who, to the cautious dismay of their elders, left their colonial schools and set off across the border to train as freedom fighters. The white state retaliated with colonial military conscription, armed the rural settlers to the teeth, and patrolled the villages with black "auxiliary" forces that hunted down guerrilla sympathizers who provided food, shelter or comfort. Peasants impoverished by growing white competition in maize and cattle farming were angrily driven into supporting the liberation forces that crossed their land by night. Zanu's popularity rose rather than fell.

The liberation war in Zimbabwe was brought to an end not by victory on the ground but by international pressure from outside. The last phase of the war was brutal, with thousands of villagers rounded up into security compounds, rural crops destroyed to deprive the guerrillas of food, and the widespread torture of detainees to obtain intelligence information. The Catholic Church began to publicize the Rhodesian terror to the outside world and break the silence of censorship that Ian Smith's government tried to maintain. At the same time South Africa, and the Western nations that had invested so profitably in apartheid, feared that the Zimbabwean armed struggle might spill over into South Africa and jeopardize its economic miracle. Internally, the Smith government was finding that the early economic benefits of independence were waning and that the costs of the war had become insupportable. It therefore tried again to end the war, this time bypassing the leaders of the parties in exile and signing an internal settlement with black politicians who had no connection with the armed struggle. Muzorewa won the ensuing election and became prime minister in 1978, but he could not offer Zimbabweans jobs, land or even peace, and the war became more intense than ever. South Africa bombed the guerrilla bases and the Western powers pressed the states that hosted the refugee camps to send Zimbabwe's military leaders, who had joined forces as a "patriotic front", to another peace conference. The peace-brokers won a settlement in which they expected the new Zimbabwean parliament to split four ways between Smith, Muzorewa, Nkomo and Mugabe, leaving plenty of room for manipulation and compromise. In practice, the internationally supervised election gave a comfortable majority to Mugabe, who became the prime minister of an independent Zimbabwe in 1980. Despite the bitterness of the war, independent political life did involve extensive co-operation. Ian Smith, the champion of white supremacy, became a loyal opposition leader, and Joshua Nkomo, the father of Zimbabwean nationalism, accepted government office under his junior rival Robert Mugabe. Ironically, it was the economic system built by Smith, and the social continuity envisaged by Nkomo, that were the hallmarks of Zimbabwe's first decade of independence and not the radical transformations that had been anticipated by Mugabe.

Mugabe's victory in Zimbabwe had owed much to the support he received from his neighbours in Mozambique. But whereas the colonial war in Mozambique was as savage as the war in Zimbabwe, the Mozambique peace that followed was short-lived and decolonization brought years of foreign destabilization and internal strife. The Mozambique colonial war, like the anti-Portuguese colonial war in Angola, began in the early 1960s when the idea of freedom was rapidly spreading into eastern and southern Africa at a time when peasants who grew the colonial crops, and especially cotton, were experiencing economic decline and oppressive taxation rather than enhanced wellbeing. Reasonably peaceful demonstrations led to violent colonial repression followed by flight into exile in a familiar cycle. Portuguese reformers tried to find moderate African leaders with whom to co-operate in a programme that would ease the worst inequalities of colonial administration. They failed, and the Portuguese army, anxious to prove itself in another colonial campaign and win economic resources and political acclaim, encouraged the development of hard-line colonial conservatism backed by military force. The African exiles, led by ivory-tower intellectuals, went down the same road towards armed confrontation. They tried to build grassroots support among the northern peasants of Mozambique, but although they could offer the long-range hope of independence, and occasionally built a few schools and clinics, they could not rebuild the Portuguese or Indian network of trading posts or provide pick-up trucks that would enable peasants to sell their crops for cash to buy such essentials as salt, kerosene, soap and cooking oil. By 1970 the first war of liberation in Mozambique had failed and its leader, Eduardo Mondlane, had been assassinated.

The second Mozambique war was led by a military leader, Samora Machel, and concentrated on winning access to the central provinces and threatening the line-of-rail to Rhodesia, the settler farms of the highlands, and the enormous hydroelectric dam that Portugal was building on the Zambezi. The dam was intended to supply very cheap electricity to the South African gold mines and thereby win

Western support for Portugal as an integrated partner in the Anglo-Saxon economic bloc in southern Africa. The nationalist challenge was too much for the professional Portuguese army and its cohorts of conscripts and so the government switched its counter-insurgent strategy to one of removing hostile peasants into barbed-wired villages, as the British had done in Kenya, and arming special black police units to terrorize the countryside as the white regime had done in neighbouring Rhodesia. As in Rhodesia it was the Catholic Church that voiced humanitarian anguish at the scale of the colonial atrocities and blunted Western sympathy for the Portuguese colonial cause. It was the Portuguese professional army, however, that brought the confict to an end by refusing to fight in a war that benefited them little when conscripts were gaining promotions at their expense, police commandos were gaining the best weapons, and the Mozambique nationalists were gaining the moral advantage. Fighting stopped after the Portuguese revolution of April 1974 and a year later Machel entered the Mozambique capital and became president of the new multiracial republic.

Installing an independent government was the first step in the decolonization of Mozambique, but as the leaders soon came to realize, the struggle had to continue. Mozambique was intensely closely integrated into the colonial fabric of southern Africa and finding opportunities for the newly decolonized black population was difficult. One hundred thousand Europeans filled virtually all the upper echelons of business and administration and a comparable number of Asians filled the middle-level posts. Africans were polarized between decision-making posts at the top level of politics and menial jobs at the bottom layer of the economy, and few had been given training or opportunity to compete in the middle. One hundred thousand black migrants worked in the gold and coal mines of South Africa, and however much the independent government abhorred the immoral exploitations of apartheid, it could afford neither to relinquish the income that they brought back home nor to create new employment for them in the subdued postcolonial economy. The large-scale farming of sugar, sisal, coconuts and tea was in the hands of foreign companies and the government did not have the financial resources or managerial talent successfully to transform them into enterprises benefiting national interests rather than foreign shareholders. Equally difficult was the decision on how to approach

Mozambique's role in providing rail and harbour services to the white regime in Rhodesia, which largely depended on them for access to the sea and foreign markets. The independence honeymoon lasted for about a year before it began to unravel and economic decolonization, both planned and unplanned, followed political decolonization.

The most courageous decision taken by the new government, and in the long run the most fateful one, was the decision to accept a United Nations instruction that no member-state should do business with Rhodesia. Mozambique closed the railway, a decision that lacked any trace of economic self-interest but was a moral gesture of African solidarity that other countries could make without cost. It deprived Mozambique of an important part of the scarce foreign revenue it needed to rebuild the nation. Rhodesia's security forces retaliated by recruiting disaffected Mozambicans and training them as sabotage units to penetrate Mozambique, destroy economic targets such as the thousands of electric pylons linking the Zambezi dam to South Africa, and foster an internal opposition movement that could challenge the ideology of black liberation and solidarity. The Mozambique Government, meanwhile, was failing to satisfy the often unrealistic aspirations of its urban supporters, failing to retain the labour skills of its white population (many of whom emigrated rather suddenly to Europe), failing to give land to ambitious peasants who did not want to be allocated to collective farms, and failing to find jobs for migrant returnees from South Africa. By 1980, when Rhodesia became Zimbabwe, Mozambique was unable to reverse its own decline. The South Africans had created alternative transport services for Rhodesia and insisted, with military force, that the new Zimbabwean Government continue to use them rather than restore the old Mozambique service industries. South Africa also took over the recruiting, arming and funding of the forces of subversion that Rhodesia had created in Mozambique, and that gradually sought foreign recognition, especially in the United States, as a national resistance front, Renamo. Attempts by Britain, anxious to regain access to its old sphere of economic influence and to end the South Africa-orchestrated civil war, did not succeed during the 1980s, but in the 1990s South African policy ceased to be dominated by military intelligence and Roman Catholic peacemakers in Italy brought about a ceasefire. The United Nations supervised Mozambique's first democratic election, which demonstrated that 20 years after independence the government could win a majority in parliament even though the opposing resistance front gained a significant following in the central provinces where it had fought hardest. Mozambique could now proceed with post-colonial reconstruction while South Africa withdrew behind its borders to solve its own problems.

In 1960 the British Prime Minister, Harold Macmillan, had gone to South Africa to explain to the parliament in Cape Town about the decolonizing process in Africa – the "wind of change" as he called it. It could be argued that decolonization did not affect South Africa as it was an independent sovereign nation, and had been since 1910. That, however, was not quite the way Macmillan saw it, and he advised the South Africans to moderate their racism and temper the colonial legacy that weighed on the black majority of the population. Historians are not agreed as to whether Macmillan's intended stance was sternly paternal, warning the local parliament of the dire consequences of not following his own path of equal opportunity for black peoples, or whether it was friendly and fraternal, advising the settlers – in case they had not noticed – that the world was changing and that to protect their interests, and also of course those of Britain, they would have to make a few tactful modifications to their policies. Whatever the intention, Afrikaner politicians were outraged at British imperial impudence in suggesting that they did not know how to handle "their natives". When, a few weeks later, the newly militant Pan-Africanist Congress organized a mass demonstration against the pass laws that controlled all aspects of black life, the police at Sharpeville decided, whether through panic, premeditation or political instruction, that they could not allow themselves to be overwhelmed by law-breakers who wanted to be arrested in order to overpopulate and burst the prison system. They therefore opened fire with live ammunition and when people began to flee they went on shooting until 69 people were dead. Within 12 months the Portuguese had treated unarmed demonstrators in like fashion in both Angola and Mozambique. The prospect of decolonization in southern Africa by constitutional bargaining and parliamentary legislation had been dimmed and both of the black political parties in South Africa turned to their military wings for salvation. These commandos, however, were no match for white security forces equipped with almost unlimited legal powers of repression and the internal black leaders of South Africa were arrested, convicted and incarcerated on Robben Island.

81

The second wave of black political consciousness in South Africa came from a new generation that was stirred in the 1970s when the national economy faltered and the young could no longer find jobs to assuage their sense of political frustration. Workers, imitating black American campaigners, boycotted the buses that carried them to and from their remote dormitory slums at exorbitant fares. Activists took to the streets to welcome the fall of the Portuguese colonial empire with the clenched salutes of African solidarity. Students reorganized themselves into a black union in the belief that they should not continue to rely on the support and sympathy of even the most radical whites but must demonstrate their own ability to plan and organize. They denied charges of reverse racism and explained their desire to escape from a mental colonization that subverted their belief in their own capabilities and damaged their self-confidence. Schoolchildren in South Africa's largest city, Soweto, rioted when they found that their schooling was preparing them for dead-end jobs, or no jobs at all. They feared that the state might further restrict their access to information by educating them in the patois of the Afrikaners rather than the language of British technical and financial opportunity. They also burnt down the beer halls that clawed back their parents' wages while lulling them into alcoholic fatalism. Some of the children were killed, some were arrested, but some fled to the now independent neighbouring countries where South African commandos hunted them down, often attacking their host communities with indiscriminate violence. By 1978 the police-based security and intelligence services were showing signs of desperation and corruption. Simultaneously a slight liberal shift in American and British politics caused these countries to demand cosmetic changes in South Africa and the surrender of Namibia to the United Nations. South Africa hit back by installing a government that was largely controlled by the army. Soon afterwards the 1979 rise in oil prices made uranium valuable again, the West stopped pressing for the decolonization of Namibia, which was a major supplier of uranium, and Britain and America reverted to electing governments that were willing to support South Africa as a bastion of anti-communism with a profitable investment climate. Decolonization of both the structures of racial control and the economics of foreign relations was postponed.

In the 1980s the army-supported government of South Africa failed to bring back the white prosperity and black subservience of the 1960s. Its policy of destabilizing Angola and Mozambique was expensive and caused increasing complaints from industry about the cost of the military budget and the excessive level of taxation. Business interests also recognized that while destabilization might close guerrilla camps, it did not create profitable export markets in the region. A civilian attempt to end military adventurism in Mozambique failed in 1984, but a much more serious challenge to the army came in 1989. A major expedition was defeated inside Angola, South Africa began to lose irreplaceable military aircraft, and rising white casualties caused disgruntlement in the normally loyal electorate, which had hitherto been protected by a smokescreen of censorship. The army lost its credibility, the white political will to repress urban uprisings faltered, investors began to remove assets, patents and manufacturing licences. At exactly the same time the Cold War came to an abrupt end with the disbanding of the Soviet Union, and the Western powers saw no further need to protect settlers from possible Russian destabilization. South Africa's white politicians adopted the classic decolonizing strategy of looking for partners among their opponents. Their first negotiations were with the nationalists of Namibia who, after a long guerrilla war on the ground and intense diplomacy at the United Nations, won a separate independence in 1990. The choice of dialogue partners inside South Africa was between the Inkatha Freedom Party, a black political party with a strongly conservative ideology but a regionally limited power-base, and the African National Congress, a party with communist sympathies but a long commitment to non-racial democracy and an appeal that reached into every region and community of the country.

The history of the Inkatha Freedom Party was closely linked to the history of apartheid and to the white endeavour to create around the fringe of South Africa separate black communities that could eventually be hived off and deprived of any aspiration to citizenship rights in the core state. The Inkatha leaders were more powerful and shrewder than the leaders of other "Bantustan" units of segregated administration. They refused to accept autonomy within boundaries that were patently designed to make their "homeland" an unviable economic entity that would be permanently dependent on South Africa for temporary migrant employment and for the supply of food and manufactured goods. Instead of accepting political autonomy they accepted investment and the encouragement of black business-

83

men who were allowed to take over rural shops and then expand into larger trading firms, transport enterprises and even manufacturing plants. Black capitalism, which had originally been discouraged to force black wage earners to spend in white-owned shops, spread to the towns and created a business class that not only had a profitable investment in the political status quo, but was also potentially opposed to the ideals of socialist equality and state services that would have to be funded by taxation. South African commerce and industry felt increasingly confident that it could do business with black capitalists. More problematic was the belief of the security services that they could work in conjunction with the Inkatha Freedom Party and arm its members with automatic weapons to defend conservative values and, more specifically, preserve the fragmented partition of the black community in South Africa. This creation of an armed, ideologically committed, regionally defined party brought severe conflict to South Africa as it moved towards constitutional reform. In Natal, the last year of the old, colonial-style, white supremacy brought virtual civil war. The opponent of the Inkatha Freedom Party was the African National Congress.

The African National Congress had been founded in 1912 to give black South Africans a voice in the new union of South Africa. The steadfast commitment of the congress was to the union of all the peoples of South Africa without distinctions of race and without the ethnic separation of territories. Apartheid and the Bantustans were direct challenges to its most cherished ideals of national integration and social equality. When the white politicians reached the end of the road and could no longer afford to repress the black majority they had to decide whether the non-racial ideals of the congress were trustworthy or whether they were the sugar-coating on an essentially black political movement. They decided to seek partnership. The Afrikaner Nationalist Party dropped its entrenched leader, who had proved unable to carry through the democratic reforms that the crisis appeared to demand, and appointed a little-known though apparently conventional new president, F. W. de Klerk. He entered into dialogue with the African National Congress, released Nelson Mandela from prison, and organized a nationwide democratic election. In 1994 de Klerk was installed as vice-president of a non-racial South Africa. Nelson Mandela became president.

Conclusion

It is worth asking what parallels may be drawn between African decolonization and the other great movements of decolonization in modern world history, and whether any had bearings on the liberation of Africa. The most tragic of colonizations, with the possible exception of Australia, was the case of North America where immigrant populations virtually replaced indigenous populations that were so marginalized and reduced as to play only a negligible role in the politics of the postcolonial nations. In Africa the indigenous populations, although sometimes badly scarred by exploitation and repression, survived to be the dominant peoples in all the decolonized nations.

The parallels in Latin America are somewhat closer, although the scale of colonial immigration, the extent of interracial mixing, and the demographic decline of the indigenous peoples were all much greater than in Africa. Only in South Africa did settler and mixed-race populations similar to those of Mexico evolve and command a position of dominance. The decolonization of Latin America in the nineteenth century was carried out almost entirely to the benefit of the white descendants of immigrants. Only in Haiti, and very much later in other Caribbean islands, did the black immigrant population gain a political role, and nowhere did native Americans win significant power except temporarily in Mexico. The campaigns for independence in Spanish America, like the campaigns of initial conquest, were largely led by military leaders, and soldiers frequently seized power subsequently. In Africa military commanders were a minority among the heroes of liberation but, as in Spanish America, soldiers frequently entered politics in the postcolonial era. They normally did so to preserve an old social order and the prestige of the armed forces rather than to bring about change and open up new economic opportunity. In Portuguese America, where the white communities were overshadowed by a large black population, decolonization was led by a branch of the Portuguese royal family. Although minor members of the European nobility occasionally served as governors in Africa, none ever aspired to create an independent regime with its colonial hierarchy intact as happened in Brazil. The one attempt at white-led decolonization in Africa occurred in Zimbabwe and that was a regime of working farmers that only lasted 15 years.

The parallels between African and Asian decolonization are closer than the American parallels, but the differences are nonetheless marked, especially in western Asia. The decolonization of the Turkish empire began with the ethnic and religious fragmentation of its European territories in the nineteenth century. Any imitation of this policy of "Balkanization" in the process of imperial retreat was seen as a great threat by African leaders anxious to gain strength through unity. The pan-African movement failed, but the successor states in Africa were defined exclusively by colonial boundaries rather than by ethnic or religious cohesion. These boundaries became the preserved frontiers of a nationalism that was primarily anti-colonial and therefore functioned within the parameters of the old colonial societies, polities and economies. In Africa even limited regional attempts at co-operation and association across old colonial borders had little success. In Asia the second phase of Turkish decolonization affected the Arab dominions, which, like the German colonies in Africa, were placed under temporary British and French control after the First World War. Arab nationalism was seen as a much more severe threat to Western "imperialism" than African nationalism. As a counter to growing republican radicalism in the Arab states, Western interests built up a neocolonial partnership with the opposing power of Iran. The empire of Iran, like the empire of Ethiopia, collapsed in tragic bloodshed when both were overthrown and their Western sponsors were driven out by violent nationalists who wreaked revenge on those seen as foreign compromisers.

Several of the Arab states that emerged from Turkish decolonization were discovered to be richly endowed with oil resources.

This wealth proved a mixed blessing and attracted various forms of foreign intervention and informal control over the postcolonial Arab kingdoms. The politics of oil in the Arab states of Asia and the black states of Africa became interlocked in patterns of production and consumption. The transnational oil companies, although keen to find supplies that were not in Arab hands, went cautiously when prospecting in Africa and only began pumping oil when they were convinced that they possessed greater power than the postcolonial states in which they operated. The largest tropical producer became Nigeria, but oil wealth had negative consequences for postcolonial development and the recycling of royalty payments led corruptly to conspicuous consumption rather than investment in jobs, infrastructure and wealth creation. Two other tropical producers, Gabon and Angola, created enclave economies that were under colonial-type technical control. Revenue fed the capital cities with imports in a manner almost resembling the ostentation of small states in the Arabian Gulf, but beyond the cities the policy caused severe neglect of the African countryside. Most of the rest of Africa consumed more oil than it produced. When in the 1970s the oil-owning nations succeeded in creating a cartel that forced the oil-producing companies to increase royalty payments Africans had to pay higher prices. Their attempts to form their own cartels of producers and match increased oil prices with increased prices for their tea, coffee, cocoa and sugar were unsuccessful. As if the problems of postcolonial choices were not difficult enough, African governments now had to manage with declining resources and increased bills for fuel and transport. In addition, the influx of petro-dollars into the Arab world created a glut of investment capital, some of which found its way to Africa and created debts that the new nations could neither afford to service nor to repay. The International Monetary Fund became the new colonial supervisor of African treasuries and began significantly to determine political choices in nominally independent nations.

Parallels between southern Asia and Africa were sometimes closer than the parallels with western Asia. In southern Asia, France and Britain dealt with princes who were often wealthier and more powerful than the great chiefs of Africa and with politicians whose voices had become insistent in the first half of the twentieth century. One of the most prominent of the Asian leaders demanding decolonization was Mahatma Gandhi, an Indian lawyer whose political career began in South Africa where he sought to obtain legal and political rights for the large community of Indian settlers in the provinces of Natal and the Transvaal. After the Second World War Gandhi's tireless popular campaigning and shrewd constitutional bargaining won concessions from Britain that led to Indian independence, although not without the violence that Gandhi abhorred and an intolerance that brought a partition of the subcontinent and his own assassination. Gandhi's ideals lived on in Africa, however, where his non-violent persuasiveness was adopted by Kwame Nkrumah of Ghana and his political methods underlay the ideals of the African National Congress of South Africa. Once non-white statesmen in southern Asia had been accorded equality with white statesmen in the dominions of the British empire, and even been permitted to adopt a republican form of government that emphasized their absolute sovereignty, it became more difficult for Britain to argue that African leaders were quintessentially different and that the decolonization of the empire did not include a programme of African decolonization. India became a republic in 1950 and Ghana gained self-government in 1951.

French policy in Asia was rather different from British policy, but the repercussions in Africa were equally close, if less benign. During the Second World War the French lost control of its colonies in Indochina to Japanese invaders. When the war was over the French wished to regain their authority but their subjects, and most notably the Vietnamese, expected new freedoms. A brief constitutional compromise achieved by Ho Chi Minh created a democratic republic of Vietnam included in a wider federation belonging to the French union. The granting of partial independence to Vietnam in 1946 was a factor causing Madagascar to seek independence in 1947, but the French refused and crushed rebellious nationalists with great force. As the demand for freedom escalated in Asia, France invested ever increasing military force in the retention of its empire. In 1954, at the battle of Dien Bien Phu, 12 French battalions were defeated by nationalist forces and the French were forced to partition Vietnam and withdraw to the south. Ho Chi Minh became a hero and word spread in the colonies that France no longer had the capacity to defend its empire. Six months later the first rumblings began in the Algerian war of liberation. In the French army the response was urgent. The moral opprobrium of having virtually lost Asia so soon after the 1940 defeat in Europe brought a passionate conviction that the military could not afford to lose Africa as well. The delay in finding a decolonizing solution in Algeria was not due just to the bitter rivalry of Algerian interests but also to the aspiration of the French army to expunge the memory of Vietnam and refuse any compromise, even when pressed to do so by one of their own men, General de Gaulle.

African decolonization can be interpreted as a European retreat determined by weakness following a debilitating Second World War and the emergence of the two new tentacular empires of the United States and the Soviet Union. But decolonization was more closely paralleled by the rise of Europe in the 1950s and its growing post-war strength than it was by its destructive agonies of the 1940s. In the immediate post-war period Europe was particularly anxious to call in all the imperial resources that it could muster to feed its people, recommission its factories and rebuild its housing stock. The large bank reserves of colonial Ghana were not used to pipe water to African villages but for metropolitan reconstruction, and the groundnut plantations of colonial Tanzania were not aimed at enriching the farming poor in Africa but at providing margarine rations in the British welfare state. Decolonization was associated with returning prosperity and the first transfer of power in the tropics coincidentally took place in 1957, the very year in which the European Economic Community was formed as the cornerstone of that prosperity. In 1961 Britain applied to join the community but France vetoed its entry until convinced in 1973 that British priorities were truly European rather than imperial. Portugal also turned north in 1974, deciding that Europe offered better prospects for wealth creation than Africa, and recognizing that more Portuguese migrants had settled in France than in the colonies. The Community subsequently created a convention, signed in Lomé in 1975, which governed commercial relations between Europe and its former tropical empires. The deal aimed to protect European industry from shortages of tropical produce and to protect Africa from destabilizing fluctuations in commodity prices. It was hardly an equal bargain and was not very different from old-style colonialism, although now practised on a multinational basis governed by Brussels.

Decolonization brought many negative images of Africa: hunger, arbitrary government, foreign exploitation and ecological neglect. But it also brought positive images. In particular it started to erase the view that blackness meant inferiority, a feeling inherited from the horrors of American slavery and subconsciously reinforced by Biblical links between darkness and evil. The slogan "black is beautiful" took root among the peoples of the worldwide black diaspora and began to convince the black peoples of Africa of their own worth after nearly a century of colonial dismissal. Black Americans made pilgrimages to Ghana and West Indians sang about Ethiopia where their hero, Ras Tafari, had become emperor and host to the Organization of African Unity. African statesmen were respectfully invited to visit Buckingham Palace and the White House, not to mention the Kremlin and the Forbidden City. African art, and especially sculpture, came to be appreciated for its own sake as well as for the stimulus it had provided to the European art of Picasso and his contemporaries. African cinema created some of the minor classics of social and political commentary such as *Xala*, depicting the colonial legacy in Senegal, and *A world apart* on the heart-rending agonies of life in segregated South Africa. At a more popular level African music developed rapidly with access to new instruments and spread during the late twentieth century as black American music had done in the 1930s. The bands of Zaire recorded their music in the most sophisticated studios of Paris and the former settlers from Angola brought African music back to revitalize the mournful popular culture of Portugal. When in the 1980s British musician Bob Geldof sang "Do they know it's Christmas?" to publicize an Ethiopian drought he triggered off a worldwide burst of charitable giving to Africa that was wholly different from the racist greed of colonialism.

While men walked tall in the new Africa, women did not always find that their aspirations had been recognized. Their voices had been heard and welcomed in the liberation struggle but when the battle was over they were often expected to return to domestic duties, as the female war-workers of Europe had found before them. When African governments tried to moderate the post-independence conflicts over policy and priority by creating single-party states in which choices would be hammered out behind closed doors, they sometimes created special party sections for women but they rarely gave women real power. Even in countries where women had been mobilized in the armed forces, and told that like the liberated women of China they held up half the sky, they were not appointed to ministries of finance or defence but only, at best, to those of welfare or education.

The ideology of women's emancipation did not match the political reality. But women in tropical Africa were rarely driven to "satanic" textile workshops or electronic assembly lines and their daughters were not sacrificed to the world sex industries with quite the same disregard for human dignity as happened in southern Asia. African women nevertheless found upward mobility difficult and access to education and the professions was very competitive. In countries where agriculture yielded low incomes the majority of women remained farmers, vegetable sellers or traders of ready-cooked foods. But it was women farmers who enabled Africa to survive the famines of decolonization by planting maize around refugee camps, growing tomatoes on the verges of city streets, and walking miles to fetch water in the absence of vehicles or pumps. These women were the invisible heroines of the African revolution.

The last question a reader will ask is whether the African revolution that led to decolonization was the result of nationalist campaigning for independence, or the result of an imperial retreat, or the consequence of superpower pressure to gain access to a continent guarded by Europeans. The answer given above is that all three factors were important. Nationalists were skilled at putting their case forward and appealing to natural justice in a post-war world where freedom was proclaimed by members of the United Nations. And the colonial powers did have new priorities in Europe that took precedence over African programmes that no longer needed an expensive imperial framework. The new world powers did aspire to shoulder Europe aside and extract wealth from Africa in partnership with new African governments that they encouraged. The changes laid a heavy burden of responsibility on Africa's politicians who had to conduct their diplomacy with partners who wielded greater power, possessed richer resources, and had more experienced civil servants than they did. In the nineteenth century the British statesman Benjamin Disraeli had claimed that "colonies do not cease to be colonies simply because they are independent". Some of Africa's proud people might sadly echo the sentiment a century later. When South Africa finally gained democracy and equality, the first state visitor to its new black president was the president of France, François Mitterrand, anxious as ever to extend French economic imperialism.

Governments in independent Africa

Country	Date of independence	Leaders since independence
Algeria	1962	Ahmed Ben Bella, 1962–5
		Col. Houari Boumedienne, 1965–78
		Chadli Bendjedid, 1978–92
		Mohamed Boudiaf, 1992
		Ali Kafi, 1992–94
		Lamine Zerouai, 1994
Angola	1975	Dr Agostinho Neto, 1975–9
		José Eduardo dos Santos, 1979–
Benin (Dahomey)	1960	Hubert Maga, 1960–3
		Gen. Christophe Soglo, 1963–4
		Sourou-Migan Apithy (Pres.),
		Justin Ahomadegbé (Vice Pres.), 1964–5
		Tahirou Congacou, 1965
		Gen. Soglo, 1965–7
		Lt-Col. Alphonse Alley, 1967–8
		Dr Emile Zinsou, 1968–9
		Maj. Kouandete, 1969
		Hubert Maga, 1970
		Sourou-Migan Apithy, 1971
		Justin Ahomadegbé, 1972
		Maj. (later Lt-Gen.) Matthieu Kerekou, 1972–91
		Nicéphore Soglo, 1991–
Botswana (Bechuanaland)	1966	Sir Seretse Khama, 1966–80
		Dr Quett Masire, 1980–
Burkina Faso (Upper Volta)	1960	Maurice Yaméogo, 1960–6
		Lt-Col. (later Gen.) Sangoule Lamziana, 1966–80

Country	Date of independence	Leaders since independence
		Col. Saye Zerbo, 1980–2
		Maj. Jean-Baptiste Ouedraogo, 1982–3
		Capt. Thomas Sankara, 1983–7
		Capt. Blaise Compaoré, 1987–
Burundi	1962	Mwami Mwambutsa IV, 1962–5
		Col. Michel Micombero, 1966–76
		Lt-Col. Jean-Baptiste Bagaza, 1976–87
		Maj. Pierre Buyoya, 1987–93
		Melchior Ndadaye, 1993–4
		Cyprien Ntaryamina, 1994.
Cameroun (French Cameroun and South Cameroons)	1960	Ahmadou Ahidjo, 1960–82
		Paul Biya, 1982–
Cape Verde	1975	Aristides Pereira, 1975–91
		Antonio Mascarenhas Monteiro, 1991–
Central African Republic (Ubangui-Chari)	1960	David Dacko, 1960–6
		Lt-Col. (later Emperor)
		Jean-Bedel Bokassa, 1966–79
		David Dacko, 1979–81
		Gen. André Kolingba, 1981–93
		Ange-Félix Patasse, 1993–
Chad	1960	François Ngarta Tombalbaye, 1960–75
		Maj-Gen. Félix Malloum, 1975–9
		Goukouni Oueddei, 1979–82
		Hissène Habré, 1082–90
		Idriss Déby, 1990–
Comoros	1975	Ahmed Abdallah, 1975
		Ali Soilih, 1975–8
		Ahmed Abdallah and Mohamed Ahmed (co-Presidents), 1978–89
		Said Mohamed Djohar, 1989–
Congo	1960	Abbé Fulbert Youlou, 1960–3
		Alphonse Massemba-Débat, 1963–8
		Capt. (later Maj.) Marien Ngouabi 1968–77
		Col. Joachim Yhombi-Opango, 1977–9
		Col. (later Gen.) Denis Sassou-Nguesso, 1979–92
		Pascal Lissouba, 1992–
Côte d'Ivoire	1960	Félix Houphouët-Boigny, 1960–93
		Henri Bédié, 1993–
Djibouti (French Somaliland)	1977	Hassan Gouled Aptidon, 1977–

Country	Date of independence	Leaders since independence
Egypt	1922	King Farouk, 1937–52 Gen. Muhammad Naguib, 1952–4 Lt-Col. Gamal 'Abd al-Nasser, 1954–70 Muhammad Anwar al-Sadat, 1970–81 Hosni Mubarak, 1981–
Equatorial Guinea (Fernando Póo and Rio Muni)	1968	Francisco Macias Nguema, 1968–79 Lt-Col. (later Brig-Gen.) Teodoro Obiang Nguema Mbasogo, 1979–
Eritrea	1994	Issaias Afewerki, 1994–
Ethiopia		Emperor Haile Selassie, 1932–74 Gen. Aman Andom, 1974 Gen. Teferi Bante, 1974–7 Lt-Col. Mengitsu Haile Mariam, 1977–91 Ato Meles Zenawi, 1991–
Gabon	1960	Leon M'Ba, 1960–7 Albert-Bernard (later Omar) Bongo, 1967–
Gambia	1957	Sir Dawda Jawara, 1965–
Ghana (Gold Coast and Togoland)	1957	Kwame Nkrumah, 1957–66 Lt-Gen. J. A. Ankrah, 1966–9 Brig.-Gen. A. A. Afrifa, 1969 Dr Kofi Busia, 1969–72 Col. (later Gen.) I. K. Acheampong, 1972–8 Lt-Gen. Frederick Akuffo, 1978–9 Flight-Lt. Jerry J. Rawlings, 1979 Dr Hilla Limann, 1979–81 Flight-Lt. (later Pres.) Jerry J. Rawlings, 1981–
Guinea	1958	Ahmed Sékou Touré, 1958–84 Gen. Lansana Conté, 1984–
Guinea-Bissau	1973	Luis de Almeida Cabral, 1973–80 Maj. João Bernardo Nino Vieira, 1980–
Kenya	1963	Jomo Kenyatta, 1963–78 Daniel T. Arap Moi, 1978–
Lesotho (Basutoland)	1966	King Moshoeshoe II, 1966–90 King Letsie III, 1990–
Liberia	1847	William V. S. Tubman, 1944–71 William R. Tolbert Jnr, 1971–80 Master-Sgt. (later Gen.) Samuel K. Doe, 1980–90 Amos Sawyer, 1990–94 War lords, 1994–
Libya (Cyrenaica, Tripolitania and Fezzan)	1951	King Idris, 1951–69 Col. Muammar Gaddafi, 1969–

Country	Date of independence	Leaders since independence
Madagascar	1960	Philibert Tsirinana, 1960–72
		Gen. Gabriel Ramanantsoa, 1972–5
		Col. Richard Ratsimandrava, 1975
		Lt-Cdr. (later Admiral) Didier Ratsiraka, 1975–93
		Albert Zafy, 1993–
Malawi	1964	Dr Hastings Kamuzu Banda, 1964–94
(Nyasaland)		Bakili Muluzi, 1994–
Mali	1960	Modibo Keita, 1960–8
(French Soudan)		Lt. (later Gen.) Moussa Traoré, 1968–91
		Lt-Col. Amadou Toumani Touré, 1991–2
		Alpha Oumar Konare, 1992–
Mauritania	1960	Moktar Ould Daddah, 1960–78
		Lt-Col. Mustapha Ould Mohammed Salek, 1978–9
		Lt-Col. Ahmed Ould Bouceif, 1979
		Lt-Col. Mohamed Khouna Ould Haidalla, 1979–84
		Col. Moaouya Ould Sid 'Ahmed Taya, 1984–
Mauritius	1968	Sir Seewosagur Ramgoolam, 1968–82
		Aneerood Jugnauth, 1982–
Morocco	1956	King Mohamed V, 1956–61
		King Hassan II, 1961–
Mozambique	1975	Samora Machel, 1975–86
		Joaquim Alberto Chissano, 1986–
Namibia	1990	Sam Nujoma 1990–
(South-West Africa)		
Niger	1960	Hamani Diori, 1960–74
		Lt-Col. Seyni Kountche, 1974–87
		Brig. Ali Saibou, 1987–93
		Mahamdou Issoufou, 1993–
Nigeria	1960	Dr Nnamdi Azikiwe (Pres.) and Sir Abubakar Tafawa Balewa (PM), 1960–66
		Gen. J. T. Aguiyi-Ironsi, 1966
		Lt-Col. (later Gen.) Yakubu Gowon, 1966–75
		Gen. Murtala Muhammed, 1975–6
		Gen. Olusegun Obasanjo, 1976–9
		Shehu Shagari, 1979–83
		Maj-Gen. M. Buhari, 1983–5
		Gen. Ibrahim Babangida, 1985–93
		Gen. Sanni Abacha, 1993–
Réunion		President of France
Rwanda	1962	Grégoire Kayibanda, 1962–73

Country	Date of independence	Leaders since independence
		Maj. Gen. Juvenal Habyarimana, 1973–94
São Tomé and Príncipe	1975	Manuel Pinto da Costa, 1975–91 Miguel Trovoada, 1991–
Senegal	1960	Léopold Sédar Senghor, 1960–80 Abdou Diouf, 1981–
Seychelles	1976	James Mancham, 1976–7 France-Albert René, 1977–
Sierra Leone	1961	Sir Milton Margai, 1961–4 Sir Albert Margai, 1964–7 Siaka Stevens, 1967 Brig-Gen. David Lansana, 1967–8 Brig-Gen. Andrew Juxon-Smith, 1968 Siaka Stevens, 1968–85 Gen. Joseph Saidu Momoh, 1985–92 Capt. Valentine Strasser, 1992–
Somalia (Italian Somaliland and British Somaliland)	1960	Aden Abdulle Osman, 1960–7 Abdi Rashid Ali Shirmake, 1967–9 Maj-Gen. Mohamed Siad Barre, 1969–90 War lords, 1990–
South Africa	1910	Jan Smuts, 1939–48 D. F. Malan, 1948–54 J. G. Strijdom, 1954–8 Dr Hendrik Verwoerd, 1958–66 B. J. Vorster, 1966–78 P. W. Botha, 1978–89 F. W. de Klerk, 1989–94 Nelson Mandela, 1994–
Sudan	1956	Ismail el-Azhari, 1956 Abdullah Khalil, 1956–8 Gen. Ibrahim Aboud, 1958–64 Sayed Sir el-Khatim el-Khalifa, 1964–5 Mohamed Ahmed Mahgoub, 1965–9 Col. (later Gen.) Gaffar Mohamed Nimeiri, 1969–85 Gen. Abdulrahman Swareldarhab, 1985–6 Ahmed Ali Al-Marghani, 1986–9 Lt-Gen. Omer Hassan Ahmed el-Bashir, 1989–
Swaziland	1968	King Sobhuza II, 1921–82 Queen Mother Indlovukazi Dzeliwe, 1982 Queen Regent Indlovukazi Ntombi, 1983–6 King Mswati III, 1986–

Country	Date of independence	Leaders since independence
Tanzania (Tanganyika and Zanzibar)	1961	Julius K. Nyerere, 1961–85 Ali Hassan Mwinyi, 1985–
Togo	1960	Sylvanus Olympio, 1960–3 Nicolas Grunitzky, 1963–7 Lt-Col. (later Gen.) Etienne Gnassingbe Eyadema, 1967–
Tunisia	1956	Habib Bourguiba, 1956–87 Zine El-Abidine Ben Ali, 1987–
Uganda	1962	King Mutesa II, 1962–6 Milton Obote, 1966–71 Gen. (later Field Marshal) Idi Amin Dada, 1971–9 Yusufu Lule, 1979 Godfrey Binaisa, 1979–80 Paulo Muwanga, 1980 Milton Obote, 1980–5 Tito Okello, 1985–6 Lt-Gen. Yoweri K. Museveni, 1986–
Western Sahara (Spanish Sahara)	(1975)	In dispute
Zaire (Belgian Congo)	1960	Joseph Kasavubu (Pres.), 1960–5 PMs: Patrice Lumumba, 1960 Joseph Ileo, 1960–1 Cyrille Adoula, 1961–4 Moïse Tshombe, 1964–5 Evariste Kimba, 1965 Gen. Mobutu Sese Seko, 1965–
Zambia (Northern Rhodesia)	1964	Kenneth. D. Kaunda, 1964–91 Frederick J. Chiluba, 1991–
Zimbabwe (Southern Rhodesia)	1980	Robert G. Mugabe, 1980–

After Ali Mazrui, UNESCO *general history of Africa*, vol. 8 (Heinemann), David Crystal, *The Cambridge encyclopedia*, 2nd edn, and *Africa Confidential* (fortnightly).

Select bibliography

Achebe, C. *A man of the people* (London: Heinemann, 1966).

Ageron, C-R. *Modern Algeria* (London: Hurst, 1991).

Ajayi, A. J. F. & M. Crowder. *History of West Africa*, vol. 2 (Harlow: Longman, 1974).

Austen, D. *Politics in Ghana* (Oxford: Oxford University Press, 1964).

Austen, R. *Africa in economic history* (London: Currey, 1987).

Austen, R. & R. Headrick, Equatorial Africa under colonial rule. In *History of Central Africa*, vol. 2, Birmingham & Martin (eds) (Harlow: Longman, 1983).

Bayart, J-F. *The state in Africa* (Harlow: Longman, 1993).

Beinart, W. *Twentieth-century South Africa*. Oxford, Oxford University Press, 1994.

Berman, B. & J. Lonsdale, *Unhappy valley: conflict in Kenya and Africa* [2 vols] (London: Currey, 1992).

Biko, S. *I write what I like* (London: Heinemann, 1978).

Birmingham, D. *Frontline nationalism in Angola and Mozambique* (London: Currey, 1992).

Birmingham, D. *Kwame Nkrumah* (London: Sphere, 1990).

Birmingham D. & P. M. Martin (eds), *History of Central Africa*, vol. 2 (Harlow: Longman, 1983).

Boahen, A. A. *Topics in West African history* (Harlow: Longman, 1986).

Boyd, B. *Brazzaville Beach* (Harmondsworth: Penguin, 1990).

Crowder, M. *Cambridge History of Africa*, vol. 8 (Cambridge: Cambridge University Press, 1984).

Crowder, M. *Senegal: A study in French assimilation policy* (Oxford: Oxford University Press, 1962).

Darwin, J. *The end of the British empire* (Oxford: Blackwell, 1991).

Davidson, B. *The black man's burden: Africa and the curse of the nation-state* (London: Currey, 1992).
Davidson, B. *No fist is big enough to hide the sky* (London: Zed Press, 1981).
Davidson, B. *The search for Africa* (London: Currey, 1984).
de St Jorre, J. *The Nigerian civil war* (London: Hodder & Stoughton, 1972).
Dunn, J. *West African states* (Cambridge: Cambridge University Press, 1978).
Fieldhouse, D. K. *Black Africa, 1945–1980* (London: Allen & Unwin, 1986).
Flint, J. *Nigeria and Ghana* (Englewood Cliffs: Prentice Hall, 1966).
Gifford, P. & W. R. Louis, *Decolonization and African independence* (New Haven: Yale University Press, 1988).
Hargreaves, J. *Decolonization in Africa* (Harlow: Longman, 1988).
Hargreaves, J. *The end of colonial rule in West Africa* (London & Basingstoke: Macmillan, 1979).
Holland, R. F. *European decolonization* (London & Basingstoke: Macmillan, 1985).
Hopkins, A. G. *An economic history of West Africa* (Harlow: Longman, 1973).
Horne, A. *A savage war of peace: Algeria 1954–1963* (London: Macmillan, 1987).
Hrbek, I. North Africa and the Horn. In UNESCO *general history of Africa*, vol. 8, A. Mazrui (ed.) (Oxford: Heinemann, 1993).
Iliffe, J. *A modern history of Tanganyika* (Cambridge: Cambridge University Press, 1979).
Isichei, E. *A history of Nigeria* (Harlow: Longman, 1983).
Kanogo, T. *Squatters and the roots of Mau Mau* (London: Currey, 1987).
Kapuscinski, R. *The emperor* (London: Quartet, 1983).
Kapuscinski, R. *Another day of life* (London: Pinter, 1988).
Malan, R. *My traitor's heart* (London: Bodley Head, 1990).
Marks, S. *The ambiguities of dependence in South Africa* (Baltimore: Johns Hopkins University Press, 1986).
Marks, S. *Divided sisterhood* (London & Basingstoke: Macmillan, 1994).
Marsot, A-S. *A short history of modern Egypt* (Cambridge: Cambridge University Press, 1985).
Martin, P. M. *Leisure and culture in colonial Brazzaville* (Cambridge: Cambridge University Press, 1995).
Mazrui, A. (ed.). UNESCO *general history of Africa*, vol. 8 (Oxford: Heinemann, 1993).
Mazrui, A. & M. Tidy, *Nationalism and new states in Africa* (London: Heinemann, 1984).

Middlemas, K. *Cabora Bassa* (London: Weidenfeld, 1975).

Morris, R. *Uncertain greatness* (New York, 1977).

Newitt, M. *A history of Mozambique* (London: Hurst, 1995).

Nkrumah, K. *Ghana, an autobiography* (London: Nelson, 1957).

Nkrumah, K. *Revolutionary path* (London: Panaf, 1973).

O'Brien, D. C. et al., *Contemporary West African states* (Cambridge: Cambridge University Press, 1989).

Oliver, R. & J. D. Fage, *A short history of Africa,* 6th edition (Harmondsworth: Penguin, 1988).

Ousman, S. *God's bits of wood* (London: Heinemann, 1970).

Ranger, T. Settlers and liberators in the south. In *History of Central Africa,* vol. 2, Birmingham & Martin (eds) (Harlow: Longman, 1983).

Rathbone, R. *Murder and politics in colonial Ghana* (New Haven: Yale University Press, 1993).

Ruedy, J. *Modern Algeria* (Bloomington: Indiana University Press, 1992).

Rooney, D. *Sir Charles Arden-Clarke* (London: Rex Collings, 1982).

Spínola, A. *Africa and the future* (Lisbon, 1973).

Sykes, J. *Africa and Portugal* (London: Hutchinson, 1971).

Thompson, L. *A history of South Africa* (New Haven: Yale University Press, 1990).

Twaddle, M. The struggle for political sovereignty in eastern Africa. In *UNESCO general history of Africa,* vol. 8, A. Mazrui (ed.) (Oxford: Heinemann, 1993).

Urdang, S. *And still they dance* (London: Earthscan, 1989).

wa Thiong'o, N. *A grain of wheat* (London: Heinemann, 1968).

Young, C. *Politics in the Congo* (Ithaca: Princeton University Press, 1965).

Zewde, B. *A history of modern Ethiopia* (London: Currey, 1991).

Index